# The Real World of
# 1984

# The Real World of
# 1984

## A Look at the Foreseeable Future

■ ■

## Richard N. Farmer

*David McKay Company, Inc.*

NEW YORK

Part of Chapter 3 was originally published, in a slightly different form, in
an article entitled "Death of Cities" in *MSU Business Topics* in 1971 and is
reprinted by permission.

*Library of Congress Catalog Card Number: 73-84057*

*ISBN: 0-679-50431-1*

MANUFACTURED IN THE UNITED STATES OF AMERICA

To

*Chris*
*Jeff*
*Sarah*
*Dan*

Who will inherit the real world of 1984

# *Preface*

A long time ago, George Orwell wrote his brilliant book *1984*, and since then this year has had a mystical significance for many people. 1984 is the doomsday year, when everyone is a slave, when Big Brother will be watching, and when no one can call his soul his own. It is a shock to realize that *the* year is only a decade away. Instead of being way out there in the misty future, many of us will live to see what 1984 is really all about.

Orwell wrote in the doomsday tradition. Everything is in tough shape and getting worse. Many writers and prophets, good and bad, have eagerly extended his literary and scientific prophecies. In the end we are all doomed to be slaves in some technocratic civilization, if indeed we aren't slaves already. Anyone picking up a modern American newspaper or newsmagazine can find enough gloom and despair, to say nothing of forecasts of worse to come, to terrify even the most optimistic citizen.

But, as someone once said, "If things are so bad, why do I feel so good?" This author happens to feel pretty good, and it seems that when one wanders around the odd corners of the republic, lots of citizens, including many who really believe the doomsday forecasts, appear to be having lots of fun. Something terrible will happen for sure, but meanwhile, let's stagger on. This peculiar optimism seems worth investigating.

Orwell invented the slogans which turn the world around. Freedom is slavery; strength is weakness; honesty is corruption. But one development in modern life which gets much less attention than it deserves is that this turning around of words can be put backward. Many argue that we are slaves—but one man's slavery may well be another's freedom. What one person sees as evil pandering to mass taste might well be another man's fine art. All is in the perception of the observer, and most articulate observers are not average people. They tend to be highly intelligent commentators reflecting their own views of what utopia should be.

My own argument is that our real problem now, and much more so for 1984, is that we are getting freer too fast. Since most people most of the time will choose what they perceive to be freedom and flexibility over what is less free and less flexible, we can forecast what the real world of 1984 will be like. It will be the sum of choices made by millions of people about their own personal freedom. If these choices seem perverse to many observers, this is too bad—we will just have to learn to live with them, or try to impose some sort of police state which forces people to take options they wouldn't otherwise.

Most of us, including me, have an irresistible urge to brainwash those misguided people out there. If only they *really* understood what was going on, they would make better choices and behave the way nice people (like you and me) behave. Any book is an effort to change behavior, and this one is no exception. When we see weird and sometimes irrational choices being made, we get frustrated, particularly when those choices put us in a worse position, in terms of income, power, or prestige, than we feel we deserve. This point really explains why we read and hear so much about doomsday—if I am losing out relatively, obviously the world is going astray. Something must be done to get us back in line, and that something involves the rest of you, not me.

But the rest of the people just nod, smile, and go right on making the same foolish mistakes. This book got started one dark night when it occurred to me that just possibly those "fools" might be displaying a bit more common sense and insight than many critics. After all, normal people rarely destroy themselves. If what they are doing is painful to planners, thinkers, utopia builders, social commentators, and other doomsday prophets, then such thinkers will have to resolve their own problems.

So, welcome to one man's real world of 1984. It is not the doomsday version, although, as you will see, it is not exactly anyone's utopia either. Rather, it is like most of human endeavor—a bit messy, full of fun, problems, disasters, issues, amusements, and conflict. Most of all, it is full of 215 million people trying to get along in a confusing world, which is never as bad as it sometimes appears, but never as good as we would like.

*Richard N. Farmer*
TORONTO
MAY 1973

# Contents

# 1

■ ■

## *The Real World of 1884*

Lem Jackson was carefully finishing off the second, larger grave he had dug in the rocky southern Indiana soil. He had had practice; there were two older graves in his family plot in the churchyard, for his two children who had died in the typhoid epidemic of '81. He glanced at the sun's position and hastily finished off the final corner. The parson would be along soon, and the funeral would take place in the church behind the graveyard. In 1884, embalming was well known, but little practiced in rural areas, and bodies were laid away hastily. Already it had been over two days.

The gravestones were lying beside the holes Lem had dug.

Lucinda Moore Jackson
June 4, 1853
March 11, 1884

John Peter Jackson
March 10, 1884
March 11, 1884

Lem gazed down at them, wiping his mouth. He had
wanted to put a nice inscription on his wife's tombstone,
but he just couldn't afford it. As it was, the two stones
cost him six dollars, and he had to scrape to get that. He
heard the squeak of the parson's carriage—old fool
never did grease the axles—and he turned to go to the
church and the funeral.

It was a quiet, bitter day in March in 1884, and life
went on as usual. Lem thought of the cows at home to
milk, seven miles away. With luck, he could get back
before dark in his steel-tired wagon. The roads were
flooded around Pollits Crossing, but he had gotten
through this morning, and he could probably get
through again this afternoon. With a bit of luck, he could
cover the seven miles in a little over two hours.

Lem's wife had been feeling poorly during the last
month of her pregnancy—her teeth were bothering her
badly, and she seemed listless and pale. Lem worried,
but he couldn't do much else. Even Doc Benton, who
took a look at her when they were in town in February,
didn't know what was the matter. Maybe he should have
done something, but no one in 1884 knew what to do.
Louis Pasteur and many others in Europe and the United
States were working on strange new ideas about bacteria
and infection, but such knowledge was not available to
Doc Benton in rural Indiana. His pharmacopoeia was not
much different from a Roman physician's eighteen hundred years earlier. So a few friends and neighbors gathered, the funeral was held, and two plain wooden coffins,
one large, one very small, were lowered into the rocky
ground. Lem and his neighbors covered them up,

mounted the gravestones, shook hands somberly, and started for home over the rutted dirt tracks of the rural America of 1884. It was a typical day of the era.

The rituals of birth, marriage, death, and recycling had changed little in a thousand years. Lem was closer to A.D. 1 than to 1973. Oh, he had a coal-oil lamp (kerosine) instead of candles; his wagon had horse-collars and a fifth wheel; his clothes had been woven on power looms and sewn on sewing machines; and he had a horse-drawn reaper at home that could do the work of twenty men with scythes, but his life style was still that of one accustomed to hard work, farm life, early death, and few expectations. The birthrate was almost forty per thousand, or what it now is in the very poor countries, and the death rate was over twenty-five per thousand—or perhaps twice what it now is even in very backward regions of the world. Lem's farm was an animal-powered operation, like all farms of that day. A few tinkerers were beginning to use steam engines for threshing, but such goings-on were reserved for a few eccentrics. The machines were too cumbersome and too expensive to be very practical.

Lem had privacy for sure, more of it than he really wanted. His two or three close neighbors were the only people he saw from week to week, unless he took the seven-mile run to town—which took most of a day. Once in town, he could take a train—the 1880s were a decade of frenetic railroad construction, and that was a new thing. In spite of much grumbling about high rail-rates, farmers in the area were now linked to international markets for the first time, and since the railroad had been built in 1882, farms were changing rapidly from almost total self-sufficiency to a market economy. Lem's own standard of living had gone up very rapidly in the past two years—his cash income had moved from under thirty dollars a year to almost two hundred. Indeed, he had

bought his wife a sewing machine only four months ago.
She had been pleased, too, and the shirt he was wearing
she had made on her new Singer.

But Lem had no telephone (the first ones were invented in 1876, and no company yet served this remote
village); no electricity (dynamos were in use in a few
places, but major uses of electricity were still ten years
off; the first two miles of electric railroad were to go into
service in Baltimore in 1885); no phonograph (the first
models were sold, at high prices, in 1886); and probably
no toilet paper (the perforated toilet paper roll was patented in 1880). Sitting in his windswept outhouse after
milking the cows, Lem could be thankful that his false
teeth were usable—the first really workable ones came
along around 1864—and that his wife had the blessing
of chloroform as an anesthetic in her fatal illness.

Lem was a middle American of his time, a time when
there were lots of births, plenty of deaths, diseases
around that no one has ever even seen recently, such as
typhoid, cholera, and diphtheria. Half of all Americans
lived on farms in a type of isolation and poverty that few
modern Americans can even conceive of, let alone have
experienced. Lem received his weekly county paper, a
four-page job hand set on a small press (the linotype
machine didn't appear until 1890). And that was all the
information he received. No radio, of course, nor any
other way, except word of mouth, to receive information.
Blaine was to run against Cleveland in the presidential
election of 1884, but for all it mattered to Lem, the
candidates might as well have been on the moon. Local
government had set up a one-room schoolhouse for
Lem's two surviving children, and it also kept track of
land titles and deeds. National government fiddled with
tariffs, but Indiana was a long way from Washington, and
there was little the federal government did which could
make any difference at all to Lem. He received no subsi-

dies, didn't get drafted, and got no services (not even rural free-mail delivery—which would come in the 1890s).

Lem was lonely in a way few modern Americans would understand. His farm was animal- and human-energy-powered, which is another way of saying that he worked hard from dawn 'til dusk to get a pathetically small crop for his pains. It also meant that he had no time to go to town, to interact even with his neighbors, let alone more distant people. Seven days a week, 365 days a year, he labored, as men and women had labored for millenia, and not once did he think it strange that this was the way the world worked. He was shrewd and observant, like so many men of his time, but by modern standards, incredibly ignorant. The seepage from his outhouse would work into his well, and the kids would get typhoid; no one anywhere knew why this was so or what to do about it. Lem was sluggish in winter, because his diet was flour and dried meat—canning on a big scale was yet to come, although food preservation was one of the growth industries of the 1880s. But transportation and communications were the real limiting factors. The 1880s were boom years for railroad construction—every hamlet in the country desperately desired the rails, because they exploded distance. Rail transport cost perhaps 1.5 cents per ton mile (or perhaps 5 cents in today's purchasing power), while the best horse-drawn wagons, operating on reasonably good roads, could not haul for less than 15 cents per ton mile. If your town had a railroad and a telegraph office, as Lem's had in the early 1880s, you could join the world. But a cable was so expensive that only the really critical messages were sent, such as agricultural market prices and death notices, and few folks traveled far at costs of 2 cents a passenger mile (say, 8 cents at today's prices), when per capita incomes were under four hundred dollars per year. Lem himself had

never been out of his county, and he never really expected to. Travel was uncomfortable, expensive, and
enervating, and on his income there was no place to go
in any case.

Lighting his coal-oil lamp with a safety match (around
since 1833), Lem picked up his newspaper and began to
read. The panic of '83 was over—there was a building
boom in Chicago. Maybe that was someplace to go—
after all, his cousin John now worked for the railroad
shops in Chicago, and he made eleven dollars a week!
Maybe he should chuck the farm and get to the big city.
He knew some blacksmithing; surely a skilled man could
do well in the burgeoning cities. But John, in writing one
of his rare letters last year, hadn't seemed all that excited
about the city. What could a poor man do, anyhow?

Lem shooed his two children to bed and turned off the
lamp. Coal oil cost big money—something about the
trusts monopolizing supply—and he didn't have much
money. He stared into the wood-fueled fireplace in his
three-room house, feeling for the first time since
Lucinda died how completely alone he was and would
be. It was incredibly quiet out there in the Indiana hint-
erland—no sounds except the rustling winds, no lights,
no activity at all. And Lem was alone, alone in the way
only nineteenth-century American farmers knew, out
someplace in the middle of nowhere, the nearest neighbor a half-mile away, with no one to talk to, no amusements to distract, nothing. Lem sighed and started to
bed. Tomorrow the fences needed mending, and soon
the plowing would start for the next year's crop, and he
had noticed that the harness was frayed and his chicken
coop needed work. He would be up at dawn for another
hard day's work, the same as he had been for the past
thirty years, ever since he was ten. With luck, he had
another twenty years or more of the same before this
world's work was done. With lots of luck—life expect-
ancy in 1884 was about forty-two years.

Lem paused and picked up the family Bible, sighed, and carefully wrote down the two entries on the flyleaf. He idly turned the pages, found Job, and read, as he and Lucinda always did. It was the only book in the house.

> My soul is weary of my life; I will leave my complaint upon myself; I will speak in the bitterness of my soul.

And farther down the page:

> Thou knowest that I am not wicked; and *there is* none that can deliver out of thine hand.
> Thine hands have made me and fashioned me together round about; yet thou dost destroy me. . . .
> Wherefore then hast thou brought me forth out of the womb? Oh that I had given up the ghost, and no eye had seen me!

Lem leaned back in his chair and prayed hard, because there was nothing else to do. The world was harsh, and God was wrathful, but this was the way the real world of 1884 was.

It was noisy enough in Chicago, even at six o'clock in the morning, when the factory whistles began to blow. Iron-tired wagons scraping along cobblestone streets made huge noises. Cousin John rolled out of bed in his three-room cold-water flat and dressed for work. His wife was already up, worrying about their six-year-old, who was coughing ominously. The place was cold—no central heating, and the coal-fired stove was tossing off clouds of acrid smoke as usual.

John, the more or less typical, city-inhabiting, middle American of his time, had his own troubles. He was tired

—working his usual sixty-hour week was all right, but he had hurt his back picking up some steel bars a month ago. He just couldn't take time off to rest it: he needed the money he earned too much. Eleven dollars a week was very good money, but it never seemed quite enough to go around, not with five kids to worry about and one on the way. He went out back to the outhouse (unknown to him, about that time in London the first practical water-control toilet was being demonstrated by Thomas Crapper; John wouldn't see one for many years). His breakfast of porridge and coffee finished, John began to walk to the shop to work. A cable car, new last year, ran out to the plant, but the walk was only three quarters of a mile, and John needed the nickel.

The streets were mud or cobblestones, and it was hard to figure out which was worse. The mud oozed over the stone sidewalks when the town was wet, and the noise the cobblestones created was hard to take. But the walk wasn't bad, even on a chilly March day. Everyone was close together—in a world without cars or even electric streetcars, mobility was very limited. A few wealthy people lived outside of town and commuted in by steam train, but workingmen never did.

Where the pitifully short sidewalk ended, John walked alongside the road, avoiding the piles of horse manure. The city should do more about that, he thought, swatting one of the numerous flies, since the number of horses seemed to go up every year. Most were hauling work wagons, not carriages—few people could afford the upkeep of a carriage. True, you could buy a good buggy for sixty dollars, but keeping a horse in the city meant a pile of money to feed it all year round. Not one family in a hundred could do that. So the workingmen walked, rode the railed horsecars, or took the few cable-car lines that were around. There was talk of some new electric trams, but no one in Chicago had yet seen one. Maybe they would be quieter than those wagons!

John worked in a fabricating shop the railroad owned, making and repairing car parts. It was a six-story brick building, with a huge steam engine in the basement giving power to all the equipment. Built just a few years earlier, it was a modern structure, complete with gas lighting. John went up to the third floor, examined his lathe, took out his tools, and tightened the belts to get the lathe going. Then, for five straight hours, he turned small brass rods to shape for fitting on freight cars. A half hour for lunch, and then five more hours at the lathe. He was a skilled man, and the pay was good. With luck, he'd be making twelve dollars a week in a year or two. He could last, too—his machine was well lighted with a good gas jet, and being on the third floor as he was, the fumes from the burning coal downstairs didn't bother him too much. Ten hours a day, six days a week, fifty-two weeks a year—he knew his work, and he was content.

The factory building was new because no one could have structured it the way it was built without freight elevators, which only had been around for fifteen years. In 1884, you needed to have a compact plant, because the only prime movers, powered by either steam or water, were big and clumsy. To power lots of machines at once, you went up, not out and sideways. This organization was great for workers too, since they were immobile and could not travel very long distances to work. And to get the coal into the plant in quantity at low prices, the factory had to be adjacent to a railroad. The railroad brought in the raw materials, and it took out the finished product. Industrial and commercial America in 1884 was strung out along the tracks, because there was no place else to go. Earlier, it had been strung out along the rivers and harbors, but in 1884 the railroads were rapidly taking over.

John was lucky because he was in a booming, high-growth industry. There were 125,000 miles of railroad in America in 1884—only four years earlier there had been just 92,200 miles, and by 1890, there would be 165,000 miles. John would work steadily for as long as he could. And, at thirty-eight, he could expect at least a few more good years before ill health, an industrial accident, or some other act of God stopped him. The pay was above average, and since employment was rising fast, he could expect to keep his job.

John had four years of formal schooling, which was about average for his time. He left the farm at fourteen, found an apprentice position with a blacksmith near Chicago, and gradually learned his trade. By the time he was eighteen, he was a full-fledged worker for the railroad.

Chicago was a hustling town in those days. The population had soared from 600,000 in 1880 to 750,000 in 1884. Civic boosters were predicting a million or more by 1890. A part of this growth was accidental—most railroads had, for financial or legal reasons, stopped when they reached Chicago, and it was a logical place to do shop work, build terminals, and carry on various other types of railroad work. Factories using products shipped in by rail, such as meat packing, then discovered it was a convenient place to do processing. Some of the reasons for the growth were geographical—the city tied nicely into the Great Lakes waterways system, and the docks were busy all the time. And of course Chicago was nicely suited to supply midwestern farmers with everything they needed: farm machinery was big even in 1884.

With over 750,000 active and hustling people, Chicago was where it was at. There was live entertainment of every sort, plenty of gin mills and saloons, gambling, prostitutes, and other nice and not so nice forms of pleasure. A rich man could buy a carriage, plenty of books, even a phonograph, have gas lighting and running water in his house, and even, maybe next year, contemplate getting a telephone. (The company was just getting started, as was the electric-power company.) He could send telegrams to distant friends, relatives, and business associates, even in England, since the Atlantic cable was completed. He could take a train all the way to San Francisco or to New York in tolerable comfort, get a tooth filled or extracted by a modestly competent dentist, and even with luck survive surgery. And more was to come! For the workingman like John, the world was full of wonders he couldn't afford, but few people paid much attention to the workingman.

Actually, things were beginning to happen all over, as technology was beginning to be exploited. Steam was still king, but electric power could now be generated, and it was only a matter of time until clean energy could be had cheaply. Europeans like Otto and Benz already had working models of gasoline engines, and tinkerers everywhere, including Chicago, were experimenting with horseless carriages. Visionaries and eccentrics, seeing phonographs, telephones, and telegraphs, were talking about the possibilities of having music piped into every home. For the half of all Americans living out on the farm, such wonders were still very rare, although most of them had ridden or seen railroad trains, worked with horse-drawn farm machinery, and maybe even bought their wives a sewing machine as Lem did.

But the world already, in 1884, had restructured itself for change. The components were there for the new era, crude, inefficient, and unreliable, but there, nonetheless. Lem could not visualize them, sitting on his remote farm; John could see them, and even help make them, but he also could not visualize how they would change him. Already, though, the big city had been made possible. Railroads could sweep the hinterlands of the food, fuel, and fibers necessary to supply a half million or more people crowded tightly together in a city. What the rails could not do, steamboats could. And the telegraph al-

ready had tied the United States and Europe together in
a net of instantaneous communication. Starting in a major way around 1830, with workable steamboats and railroads, transportation and communication costs had
been dropping very rapidly. It was beginning to make
sense to specialize, and John could make a single part on
his lathe, get paid, and use his pay to buy from others
what he needed to survive. Lem still did most all the jobs
himself, but he too was being slowly locked into the
specialization net, growing corn for the city in exchange
for machinery and cloth for his family. The world would
never be the same again. It was the era of the city.

What goes in, comes out, one way or another. Big
cities not only needed tons of food, clothing, fuel, and
raw materials, but they also needed to get rid of the
garbage, sewage, and smoke. The smoke was easy—just
let it blow away. If citizens breathed too much of it, it was
their problem, not the cities'. Sewage was harder, since
failure to remove waste meant pestilence and epidemics.
The rapid growth of really big cities coincided, not acci-
dentally, with major improvements in sanitation and hy-
draulic engineering. He who lived along a modern sewer
line in 1884 lived a longer and happier life. It smelled
less, and besides, fewer people got sick. And garbage
collection was easy—there was very little of it. Nothing
got wrapped—paper was still very expensive, and if you
had any, it got used to start your coal or wood fires;
canned goods were very scarce, so few cans were around;
and on wages of six to twelve dollars a week, everything
got eaten. Poor societies don't throw much away, so
garbage collection in a well-organized city was minimal
and reasonably effective.

Everything led to highly dense, compact cities, with
very high populations per square mile. Sewers cost
money, and there was little enough of that to spread
around; railroads don't like to build sidings everywhere,

and moreover, their repair and terminal work is concentrated; steam engines lead to compact multistory factories; and workers walked to work. Just go to today's inner cities, the ghettos, and look around. Some of the old brick warehouses, which used to be factories, go back to the 1880s, and plenty of housing does too. Take in the narrow streets, the crowded flats, the intensive use of land on all sides. Take a look, too, at the older upper-income housing, the moldering mansions now converted to boardinghouses, with their tight lots, carriage houses, and signs of affluence in the form of moldings and scrolls (bandsaws only became practical in the 1880s, and like most other intriguing inventions, people began to use them, which is why the scrollwork in the 1880s and later became so ornate; before then, no one could do this sort of work). Note particularly where the gentry lived—right at the edge of the central city, where a solid, prosperous merchant or manufacturer could easily stride off to work. And if you can get inside the house, note how it was designed to be labor intensive—there were plenty of low-paid Irish serving-girls available to do the work. Rapidly rising labor costs over long periods of time have made white elephants of most of the interesting large houses of the 1880s and 1890s.

By 1900, the pattern of the world which we still dream of and maybe even yearn for was complete. The electric streetcars had come to extend the cities along the tracks, and the workingman's income had risen to the point where he could ride to work from his house perhaps four or five miles away. Cities had electricity, although steam was still king in most factories. The railroads dominated intercity transportation, and the horse-drawn wagons dominated the city local transport. The gentry still used horses, but the more adventurous could buy a car. And there were even a few distant suburbs, stretched along the railroad tracks, for those who preferred the more

rustic life and could afford it. Public schools were growing fast, and kids were staying in them longer. In the
large cities, like Chicago, Boston, and New York, rapid
transit, in the form of subway, elevated, and electric
trains, sped people rapidly throughout the urban area.
Here and there electric interurbans were being built out
of cities, bringing the joys of smokeless, quiet, quick
transport even to hamlets and farms. And in a few places,
curious audiences could watch a cinescope show, where
pictures seemed to move. In 1899, Marconi actually
managed to transmit some wireless telegraph messages.
Around the same time, X rays were beginning to be used,
and while no one really understood what they were, radi-
oactivity had been discovered. It was all there in 1900,
ready for the new century. By 1900, the city, in the modern sense of the word, was a functioning organization.

But the historical landscape 1800 and even 1884, was
totally rural, simply because it was impossible, in most
places, to put many people together. Cities with populations of over a hundred thousand were very rare, and
these few were on rivers or placid seas, so that the sewage could be dumped into the water that bore sailing
ships bringing in the food and clothing that supplied the
population.

Aside from Rome, most ancient cities would be small
towns by modern standards. Many of the fabled Greek
city-states had populations approximating places like
Bedford, Indiana; or Bend, Oregon (say, ten to twenty-
five thousand). That was the maximum number of people the existing technology could support. Really big
cities are a rather recent phenonema, and in the real
world of 1884, few persons really grasped that this development was coming. Lem certainly didn't, living on his
remote farm. John perhaps sensed it, but his physical
scale was too small—he could see only what he could
walk to, which was only a small piece of 1884 Chicago.

To him the city was a cold-water flat, a multistory brick factory, a few stores nearby, maybe the corner saloon, and a church a few blocks away—what we now nostalgically call a neighborhood. It was a small four-page daily paper he bought every other day or so, an occasional book, and maybe a visit to a vaudeville house two or three times a year. It was the sound of squealing iron wagon-tires, or softly panting steam locomotives, the sight of the gentry passing by in their elegant carriages. It was a life full of hard work, disease, ignorance, and misery, along with some fun which Lem out on the farm could not know or experience. All things considered, it wasn't a bad life, but it hardly was a great one either. Mechanical slaves were beginning to replace the human and animal ones—John's lathe used a coal-fired steam engine for power, whereas the one he had learned his trade on only twenty years earlier had a boy pumping a treadle for power. John survived and even prospered a bit because steam engines were making his way of life possible.

The affluent had more fun, but there were precious few of them. In part this was because so few people really knew very much. A modern American revisiting 1884 would be shocked by the low educational levels. Out of seventy million people, only about 3 percent had high school diplomas, and less than fifteen thousand persons received college degrees annually. Men like John learned their trades the hard way, through on-the-job training, such as it was, and apprenticeships. Farmers learned by watching their fathers. Not only were people much less educated, but they were receiving perhaps one one-hundredth of the information they now receive. Many decades would pass before the new communication nets were in place to be really used.

The rural world was lonely, isolated, and private by force; the urban world was noisy, crowded, and privacy was difficult to achieve. But the affluent already were beginning to enjoy a new kind of world. One 1900 account put it this way:

Take the most matter-of-fact and prosy half hour of the day, that at the time of rising, and see what a faithful account of the average man's everyday life would present. The awakening is definitely determined by an alarm clock, and the sleepy Nineteenth Century man rolling over under the seductive comfort of a spring bed, takes another nap, because he knows that the rapid transit cars will give him time to spare. Rising a little later his bare feet find a comfortable footing on a machine-made rug, until thrust into fullfashioned hose, and ensconced in a pair of machine-sewed slippers. Drawing the loom-made lace curtains, he starts up the window shade on the automatic Hartshorn roller and is enabled to see how to put in his collar button and adjust his shirt studs. He awakens the servant below with an electric bell, calls down the speaking tube to order breakfast, and perhaps lights the gas for her by the push button. He then proceeds to the bath, where hot and cold water, the sanitary closet, a gas heater, and a great array of useful modern articles present themselves, such as vaseline, witch hazel, dentifrices, cold cream, soaps and antiseptics, which supply every luxurious want and every modern conception of sanitation. His bath concluded, he proceeds to dress, and maybe puts in his false teeth, or straps on an artificial leg. Donning his shirt with patented gussets and bands, he quickly adjusts his separable cuff buttons, puts on his patented suspenders, and, winding a stem-winding watch, proceeds downstairs to breakfast. A revolving fly brush and fly screens contribute to his comfort. A cup of coffee from a drip coffee-pot, a lump of artificial ice in his tumbler, sausage ground in a machine, batter cakes made with an egg beater, waffles from a patented waffle iron, honey in artificial comb, cream raised by a centrifugal skimmer, butter made in a patented churn, hot biscuits from the cooking range, and a refrigerator with a well stocked larder, all help to make him comfortable and happy. The picture is not exceptional in its fullness of invented agencies, and one could just as well go on with our citizen through the rest of the day's experience, and start him off after breakfast with a patented match, in a patented match case, and a patented cigarette, with his patented overshoes and umbrella, and send him along over the patented pavement to the patented street car, or automobile, and so on to the end of the day.*

This account does not bother to mention what the servant got out of all this, nor does it consider exactly how many lucky citizens had all these benefits of civilization. As has been typical of most of recorded history, the focus is on the 1 or 2 percent at the top, not on the bunch down below.

The diversions of 1884 were few and far between. Baseball was around, and some other sports were played at exclusive Ivy League schools, but the era of mass sports was still decades away. The reason was simple— no one had time or money to enjoy much of such things. The word "hobby" was yet to appear in the vocabulary —no one except a small elite had time for one. Literate people read and went to plays, if they could; others just worked, sat, and procreated. It was the way the world had always been.

*Edward W. Byrn, *The Progress of Inventions of the Nineteenth Century* (New York: Ginn & Co., 1900), pp. 458–459.

Lem and John and all the rest of the 1884ers had one thing in common—they lacked control of themselves, their life styles, their incomes, their fate in general. You would die any time from some disease or another, and no doctor knew what to do. Too many babies got born, because too few knew anything about birth control (the vulcanization of rubber had been discovered in 1839, and prophylactics apparently came along very shortly thereafter, but few men in that Victorian, less-educated world knew much about them). And no one went far on foot, on horseback, or in a wagon. If you wanted to travel, you put yourself at the mercy of a railroad. No one could afford much more than the basic necessities of life, and no one had time or leisure or education for much thoughtful contemplation. It cost more money than most people had to communicate over long distances, and amusements were few and expensive. Virtually all men were prisoners of a harsh environment, unable to do very much with themselves except struggle to survive. And, since few knew of any other kind of world, no one really worried too much about the problem. Life had always been this way, and it always would be.

In the real world of 1884, the only people that counted were male WASPs. If you were female, Catholic, black, an immigrant, Jewish, or anything else, the world belonged to someone else. Women couldn't even vote, and in most states they didn't have much in the way of human rights either. Blacks were mainly down on the farm in the south, living much as Lem did, except that most of them were poorer and less educated than even he was. And they rarely voted either, although in theory black *men* could, one "privilege" they had in contrast to a white woman.

The railroads were about the only really big companies around—most firms were small family-owned operations, so that the idea that a young, smart fellow could get a good job just by being competent was absurd. You had to have relatives to get in the game. The idea of professionalism in almost any trade was also absurd, in part because you couldn't find a job even if you had the right credentials, and in part because so little was known about so many taken-for-granted twentieth-century trades like engineering and architecture that no one really knew what to be professional about.

Immigrants were flooding the cities, and they did the dirty work for a dollar a day. Many were illiterate, most came from the bottom of their home-country social-class pyramid, and few in the first generation were able to do more than perform manual labor for low pay. But already, in 1884, they were beginning to discover that local politics yielded jobs, and in some cities they could vote. Nowadays we seem puzzled that so many local government jobs seem very important to ethnic groups (hence the Irish police or the Italian sanitation department), but few modern Americans remember just how tough it was right on into the early twentieth century for such people to crack the better part of the job market.

A change from the real world of 1884 which is just beginning to happen, and which few Americans have really thought about, is that since the beginning of major cities in the United States, there has always been another underclass to take over the dirty work for the group which just laboriously struggled out of poverty and left those dirty inner-city slums and ghettos. First the North Europeans did the dirty work for the Anglos; then the South Europeans did it for the North Europeans (which was already beginning to happen in 1884); and in some parts of the country (e.g., California), the Orientals did the same dirty work for the whites, while the blacks did it in the South. Now we see the ex-southern blacks doing what dirty work remains for us in the big cities. But the blacks are beginning to get affluent and educated too, and they are bailing out of the worst part of the inner cities just the way everyone else did. Who's the next underclass? There's no one there anymore who's poor enough and desperate enough to come. It may well be that a century of very real and brutal experience in cities may well be over by the time the real world of 1984 rolls around.

The real world of 1884 is long gone. Vestiges do remain—John's old shop stands abandoned in the Chicago inner city, and Lem's wife's grave still sits, weed-covered, in a small cemetery on a quiet Indiana blacktop rural county road. The plow Lem used sits in a suburban front yard as an interesting antique, and a black welfare mother lives with her two children in the same cold-water flat that John once rented, even though it has been condemned for several years. John's youngest son is still alive at ninety-three, out at the old Veterans' Home, and if you can get him talking, he can spin yarns about the good old days. But a man who matured in 1900, when there were under twenty-thousand cars in the country, no planes, no TV, and precious little of anything else, is himself a sort of living museum of a past long forgotten, long dead. Best to leave him in the old folks home, and worry a bit about the real worlds to come.

# 2

## What Is Freedom?

1984 has been a mystical date ever since George Orwell wrote his masterful book. And it's coming up fast, just eleven more years. By 1984, Big Brother will be watching, and the world will be totally slave. Or at least that was the way Orwell saw it. In fact, if not in fiction, the world of 1984 may just be an inviting place, filled with many options that actually increase personal freedom. But curiously, while we can find all sorts of predictions about politics, military strategies, technology, and economic development, it is difficult to find out much about how we will be living then.

Sometimes one gets the image that everything is coming unstuck. Our world is confusing, rotten, unethical, evil, and probably unviable too. One senses crisis on every hand, as one ponders pollution, ecological collapse, stinking poverty, moral decay, corruption, narcotics abuse, and a host of other ills which grow worse day by day. It is undoubtedly true that our world, like all others, has its full share of misery, but in focusing on its ills, we may just be missing what the world is all about and what it will be even more about in 1984. Somehow, in spite of everything, people are having a good time. Some of them even claim to be happy, and while everyone bitches constantly, even casual checks suggest that what he really wants is more money and more time to do what he enjoys. This reaction is hardly the cry of a doomed race.

One major reason our images are askew is that many people assume the average man is some sort of creep who should crawl back under whatever rock hides his home. It is fascinating to discover this view in literate, intelligent journals, newspapers, and magazines. Whatever the common man is doing, he is undoubtedly up to no good. Of course, there is a countering view, sometimes propounded by such people as Eric Hoffer and Tom Wolfe, that the common guy and gal actually are pretty smart. They not only know what they are doing, but they are usually enjoying it too. And this view is the one we will adopt here. Maybe eighty million Americans are wrong to buy autos or look at television, but even if they are, it might pay to examine with some care why they do these things. Unless we understand what is in the mind of the average citizen, we will never come close to understanding what our political and economic future will turn out to be. Those who fail to grasp what is really happening will never figure out the future, for better or worse. They won't win any elections, either. Be prepared: our journey takes us to some improbable and rarely discussed places, from flush toilets and model railroading to a reexamination of the auto and the city.

What makes forecasting so difficult today is that we have moved, and will continue to move, into a new kind of world, where our old models of behavior, reality, and prediction just won't work anymore. Because they don't work, we sometimes assume that all is lost. Actually, life in the real world of 1984 will probably be the freest man has ever known—and that fact alone makes us nervous. There will be life styles, differences, and power relationships unlike anything ever seen, which is why it may be fun to take a look ahead.

Not too long ago, I was listening to a city planner discuss urban problems. He was typical of the breed—intelligent, well educated, well paid, insightful. The audience also was typical—liberal, well educated, upper middle class, academics and thinkers, all nodding agreement with the wisdom of the speaker. When the planner began to talk about automobiles, his face reddened, his hands trembled, and his voice shook. He insisted that people should go back to mass transit and buses. When he finished, we gave him a nice round of applause. Then we all drifted off to the parking lot to pick up our cars. Driving home, I thought a bit about what the planner had said and what was actually happening. Bits of evidence, some insights, and the thoughts of others came to mind: Like the study in Chicago that suggested that the transit authority would have to pay a dollar or more to get a commuter to abandon his car and use the bus. Like the California study that suggested that everyone was in favor of rapid transit because the other guys would then get off the freeway and leave them uncongested for him in his own car. Like the St. Louis situation, where the poor literally tore apart a nice high-rise housing project built for them a few years back. Like my own university, where students refer to the neat, new high-rise dorms as prisons and move into an apartment which is cruddier and a lot more expensive as soon as they can. And I couldn't help thinking, as one wise young man once observed, "Never mind what people say—what are they *doing?*"

We planners have been misreading signals for a long time now. If what we think people are really up to is wildly at variance with what is actually happening in the real world, then few of our dreams are going to come true. Worse, we will end up totally discredited when our plans seldom work. The fact that confidence in government planning is apparently at an all-time low has not discouraged us—we keep right on making the same old mistakes.

My major premise is that few planners correctly perceive what most people think freedom really is. The usual perception is that freedom is dying fast, that alternatives are rapidly narrowing, and that our long-run problems stem from this fact. Actually, exactly the opposite is happening, and efforts to renew freedom in ways most people see as tyranny are doomed to fail.

## What is freedom?

Freedom is normally perceived as something political. Hence we find great debate among politicians about voting rights, political parties, government funding, and so on. But freedom to the average citizen (or even the not so average one) is typically quite different. Personal freedom for Mr. Average Citizen is seen to be increased:

a) when his vocational choices are maximized.

b) when random personal contacts are minimized: This means reducing his associations with persons whom he really doesn't care about, such as people in crowds on the street, in buses, in theaters, etc. It also includes reducing the inevitable random contacts associated with high-density living. The closer and more constant such contacts, the less personal freedom he has. Gossips may love to listen to their neighbors' domestic quarrels through thin apartment walls, but most people do not.

c) when possibilities for personal contacts of his own choice are maximized: This means selecting one's own friends and associates, Couples dating because they want to, housewives finding friends they enjoy, administrators having lunch with compatible associates, car-pool riders self-selecting companionable people, and so on. The more of this personal choice contact you have, the better off you are.

d) when the chance to do your thing, whatever this may be, is maximized: This means if you like archery, and I like antique autos, being in a position where we can both have fun at the same time.

By merely defining freedom this way we may explain why the antihero in modern American life, the suburbanite, keeps increasing in numbers. Suburban life closely meets the freedom test for a large number of people, and it is really no surprise to discover that as fast as people get enough income to go to the suburbs, they go. We all get interested in political freedom from time to time, and if someone tries to restrict it we may object. Actually we maximize our freedom by organizing our daily lives to increase our options by getting ourselves some space, a car or two, and other things more easily obtained in the suburbs than in the city. These trends are obvious to us planners, since we see them every day. But somehow, in our professional work, the image gets blurred.

We are also confused by the oft-repeated notion that things were a lot better in the past. We are haunted by images: the noble savage, the man of the tribe, roaming the wilderness, strong, self-reliant, totally free; the stalwart farmer, owning his own small plot, farming in a subsistence way, depending on no one; the laughing villager, dancing around the maypole, smiling, always happy in his small, but totally complete world. If we could only go back to those happy times when man was free. Somehow, technology has stolen our dreams from us, and because it has many thinkers believe the modern world is evil, and inevitably doomed. If we don't choke in our own effluents and exhaust emissions, the atom bomb will get us in the end. Or some other technological advance. And even if we escape that particular trap, we'll all go insane, because we can't stand the monotonous work we do, or the insipid leisure pursuits we participate in so listlessly. All is doom and despair, and it's technology's fault.

Technology and science have a bad image. About all you can say on their behalf is that virtually every human culture uses what they develop as fast as it appears, and eagerly go looking for more. What technology, science, and all the rest boils down to is fairly simple: We use nonanimal energy to get things done, in an incredible variety of ways. Productivity per man goes way up when nonanimal energy is used, since a man is a very inefficient energy system. It's a lot easier to have a gasoline-powered lift truck pick up a ton of stuff and stack it than it is to have twenty sweating laborers do it, or perhaps five men and three horses. It's a lot easier to have an electric motor roll out a steel plate, instead of having two hundred men beat out the steel by hand. It's a lot easier to have a huge mechanical shovel scoop up fifty tons of coal at one shot than to have hundreds of men do it with picks and shovels. That's all technology is, but the results, which have been hitting us for well over two hundred years now and at an accelerating pace, are lots of fun for the average man.

Technology also gives us the cheap communication systems which enlarge access to information and allow us to find out what tough shape we are in. Technology also gives us time, including, thanks to increased productivity, much more time for formal education. One of the reasons we feel so uneasy is that there are so many educated people around to think, read, and write about our problems. In earlier days, those people would be down at the plant or out on the farm working, because we just couldn't produce the economic surplus to allow more than a handful of young people access to extended educations. The point is technology makes for freedom.

Some of the instruments our technology has brought us to increase our freedom are:

*Television:* Ask anyone—freedom is seeing what you want, in the comfort of your own home, on some dark and icy night. The more channels and choices you have, the better. If you really want freedom, consider a telestar satellite parked over the United States, sending down eighty or more channels to choose from. It's possible, but it won't happen soon, largely because network executives, advertisers, government agencies, and lots of others are scared to death of the idea. Why, a fellow in Indiana might even watch a Los Angeles educational station! What would happen then to the petty monopoly of the local channel?

*The telephone:* As Ma Bell advertises, having a phone means you can contact anyone you want any time—grandma, your girl friend, your lawyer, or anyone else. Count how often a phone is used in any modern movie, play, or TV drama—this gadget is key to finding out what's going on in the world. Having access to a phone gives any human freedom of a sort only dreamed of by our ancestors. Ma Bell has the easiest marketing job ever invented—you can sell 99.9999 percent of anybody a phone without even trying. The main problem is finding enough capital and skills to get them installed.

*Electricity:* Freedom is having a 150-amp fusebox in the basement, with the income to buy the appliances (electric slaves) to use it. Ask any woman over fifty—she can remember doing dishes and clothes by hand, sweeping instead of vacuuming, worrying about rancid butter and sour milk because she didn't have a refrigerator, and hanging soggy clothes in the basement in winter instead of stuffing them in a drier. Ask any older man—he can remember handsawing wood, shoveling coal, and cranking his car. (I just counted 134 electric motors in my house, which is not too unusual these days. My 1929 house came with a 20-amp fusebox, expanded to 100 in 1955. Now it looks like it will have to be expanded to 150 or 200. I have more power on hand at the flick of a switch than a good-sized factory had in 1930.) All our electric slaves give a person time and freedom. Electricity is also available wherever the lines go, which is just about everywhere. What you get from that small copper wire is choice, freedom to do your thing.

*Autos:* Ask any teen-ager—real freedom begins the day you get your driver's license, not when you get to vote, drink, or do some other trivial thing, like get drafted. Autos are the essence of freedom—which is why we have over eighty-three million of them, with more to come. Having an auto means that you can go when you want, where you want, with whomever you want. It means that you don't have to sniff garlic in the bus, that you don't become prisoner to the railroad timetable, that you don't have to worry about strikes by transit employees, that you can live where you please. Cars mean privacy, widened vocational choice (you can get a job anywhere within ten to sixty minutes' driving time from where you live), avoiding chance personal contact, the ability to get to your thing (be it antique-auto meets or the archery club), and do what you please. Cars also mean power— the lowliest driver commands more physical power than anyone but magnificent kings did just a century ago. They also mean evasive power—if you want me to be someplace, I can get away by driving in the opposite direction. And cars mean all sorts of psychological things. Take a really close look at auto interiors: those gauges and levers and buttons and lights, to say nothing of the soft upholstery, stereo systems, radios—all images of control and freedom. Since no common carrier could come close to creating such an atmosphere, it is not surprising that most customers regard any form of public transit as inferior, including some very nice ones, like first-class airplane rides.

*Education:* Freedom is a good education, however anyone defines it. The better your education is, the freer you are to choose your vocation and avocations, and the more money you make. We tend to forget, since it happened so fast, how limited our parents or grandparents were. Median education for women in 1930 was a bit over eight years of formal schooling, which would qualify one for some drab, monotonous job in some anonymous factory. By 1965, this median had moved up to eleven-plus years. Such an education meant a clerical job, something interesting in sales, or, for the more fortunate, a professional career. Men's education followed the same pattern. Note the potential freedom—a college-trained person can work on an assembly line, but a grade-school dropout cannot perform professional or executive work. Blacks, chicanos, and other minorities—including most specifically women—understand this point only too well. Education for them, as for our WASP ancestors, means freedom and a way out. And the data on school dropouts, the number of people going to college, and similar trends suggests that most people are getting this message very well.

Education is more than just economics. It means freedom to do what only a handful of the elite have been able to do in the past, which is to explore, in whatever manner one chooses, the cultural richness of Western society, and, for that matter, all other societies. One can learn to paint, write, sculpt, or read the classics, and much of our formal education involves the arts. We often overlook the fact that sales of painting materials, books, and various forms of art have been rising rapidly for a century or more. We forget that symphony orchestras boom in improbable, provincial towns and that musical instrument manufacture is a real growth industry. Doing one's thing may well involve playing the oboe, reading Plato, listening to a classical record, or visiting an art museum, and Americans by the millions do these things every day. Such pleasures and artistic pursuits rarely come naturally —somewhere along the line, in any person's formal educational career, some gifted teacher opened these doors. The more people that have a chance at education, the more the arts will thrive. And let us not forget that education helps us use the other freedom instruments more efficiently.

*TV telephones:* Freedom will be, once we get around to installing them, TV telephones. Instead of fighting downtown traffic to get to your office so you can meet with two or three colleagues, you will sit at home (wherever you want that to be) and call them directly to see what they look like while you wheel and deal. TV telephones mean not going to grandma's for Christmas, fighting traffic and recalcitrant airline employees, but rather a quiet video chat—with all the kids getting in on the act. They mean doing business with all sorts of people at a distance, and they mean avoiding lots of random and unwanted impersonal contacts with strangers.

*Cable TV and things to your home:* Freedom will be the reception of eighty-five TV channels. It will also be, for those who want them, stock market quotations (and buying and selling, if we set up the system right), library printouts of books, weather reports, special programming for those who have unusual interests (e.g., a program for stamp collectors, bibliophiles, or whatever), and lots, lots more. And remember home can be wherever you want it to be—out in the woods or right downtown. Cable TV can include other forms of audio or visual programming too—how about printouts of newspapers or perhaps only of the parts you really want to keep? Various forms of hi-fi systems could also be included, along with some variant of Muzak. Whatever a small group wants and is willing to pay for can be provided, once the cable network is in place. Already cables are being rapidly installed by CATV systems all over the country. Much more is to come.

*Good health:* It doesn't do anyone much good to be free and sick. Having as good health as you can is a critical freedom instrument. He who has access to good dentistry, optometry, and medicine is in better shape than he who doesn't. For the one group which is most vulnerable to health problems, the aged, we already have Medicare —and similar plans are certain to come for other age groups. Good health is really freedom from debilitating illnesses and death, and we still have some ways to go before we win this battle. Indeed, for several decades now, mortality rates of people over forty haven't changed much—our gains in getting the death rate down really involve the young. A much higher percentage of those under forty live longer because of twentieth-century achievements in public health and medicine. We don't fear smallpox, polio, typhoid, malaria, and lots of other diseases that Lem had to live with in 1884. Indeed, we have been so successful that the main cause of death for those under twenty-one is accidents, followed by suicide. When you get older, new killers appear, mainly cardiovascular diseases and cancer. By 1984, we will probably have artificial hearts, plus a broad-spectrum cancer vaccine. We already are a long way down this road with today's extremely complex life-support systems for serious illnesses. But by 1984, we will have a lot more.

And, if we keep finding out more about human biology and biochemistry, we may have antiaging pills and replacement parts for virtually any human organ. We may just be on the edge of gaining both better middle-aged health and some increased longevity—which would be real freedom indeed.

American medicine is by far the most costly in the world. American medicine at its best is also as good, or better, than anyplace else. The trouble is that we can't quite figure out how to get it to all our citizens—which is why there is so much controversy over medical plans and organization. By 1984, we will have straightened out this mess. And we can look forward to a longer and healthier life. And if we do, all the other freedom instruments will be more interesting and usable.

*Birth control:* Birth control in all its forms, including abortion, is a major freedom instrument. Historically, most women were household slaves because the children came, like it or not. Now, most men and women can decide for themselves whether or not they want children, and when. The result is to free them to do whatever they want for the bulk of their lives. Incidentally, an overlooked birth-control possibility is that of *having* children if you want them, when you want them, and men may be just as interested in planned parenthood as their wives. Childless, often frustrated marriages were quite common until very recently, and the couple could do little about it. Now we have very powerful fertility techniques. The freedom to have children can be just as important as the freedom not to have them.

We also have new genetic analysis to help guarantee that children will be healthy and normal. No one wants a defective child, and today we can cut this risk. RH blood factor checks, German measles abortions, and genetic counseling are ways to help produce healthy children at the right time. And more is to come, giving still more freedom of choice. How about sex determination, specific genetic qualities built into your children? It might well come to pass before too many decades have gone by.

*Mobility:* Autos—and freeways, snow-removal systems, computerized traffic controls, and other systems to help the cars move fast—give one a sort of mobility. Thirty years ago, a fifty-mile trip on a curving two-lane highway loaded with slow trucks was about as far as anyone could go without elaborate advance preparation. Now a car can go two or three hundred miles in a few hours. A three-hundred-mile radius of action covers thirty-six times as much space as a fifty-mile radius, and our freeways are crowded with people exercising options about where to go they never had just a few years back.

But personal mobility is also a jet aircraft, with its 600-mile-an-hour speeds and low fares. You can fly coast to coast today for less dollars than it cost in 1932, even though prices generally have tripled. You can also go to Europe or the West Indies or almost anywhere on excursion rates which are incredibly cheap. Because this mobility exists, people take full advantage of it. A trip to Europe used to be something for New York millionaires —now, teen-age students, along with mechanics, retired persons on small pensions, and just about everyone else swarm by the millions all over Europe. Today more people cross the Atlantic every June than the big ships carried in a year. More cars cruise daily through Wyoming on the Interstate than used to go through the state in six months, and for that matter, even those without cars join the fun—we have all seen the battalions of hitchhikers, guitars slung over their shoulders, patiently waiting for the next ride. They get them, too.

Mobility also means finding a comfortable spot to stay when you get there. Already the international hotel system is becoming homogeneous. They all look the same, just as international airports around the world look the same. The builders of such hotels and airports realize full well that if they are to succeed, the majority of their clients have to find them comfortable, reassuring, and rather like home. Hence, they tend to be modern design.

In the old days you slept in a strange bed (or maybe on the floor), surrounded by unfamiliar things in a place which was decidedly not home. Explorers and adventurers can still find plenty of places off the beaten track, but most of us prefer something we're used to. And since tourism is a big money-maker everywhere, planners are happy to oblige. It pays because it gives people confidence that whatever happens will not be too odd or strange or frustrating.

Mobility means freedom to find out things, to visit relatives, to enjoy the High Sierras, the coastlines, and the big cities. It means being where you want to be a considerable portion of the time. Now, anyplace in the world is only thirty hours away by jet, and many desirable places are only hours away. Mobility also means much better jobs—no one is trapped in California, while the good jobs in the profession are in Illinois. You can pack up and go, and millions do, every year.

*Leisure:* Time is everyone's enemy—there is only so much of it. Lem didn't have leisure time—he worked constantly to keep his farm going and himself alive. Now, a farmer can do in two weeks what Lem did in a year, and do it much better. John worked his routine sixty-hour week in the factory in 1884, but now we get much more done in forty hours and get paid a lot more for doing it. And so we have time, perhaps the ultimate freedom instrument, since with time, we can do what we want. Some waste it and some use it for productive purposes, but at no time in human history did so many people have so many free hours as now. And the future trend will be still more leisure time. Incidentally, a major effect of many freedom instruments is time saved. Those cars mean quicker trips and time saved. Those electrical slaves do the work, leaving time to do other things. That telephone call means a trip saved. Better training means more efficient and productive work, which leads both to

getting jobs done quicker (with electrical and other mechanical slaves) and shorter work weeks.

*Putting it all together:* So what will freedom mean to the
average person (and the unusual one too, for that matter) in 1984? It will mean the expansion, often explosive,
of options. It will mean the avoidance of personal situations which are distasteful (like being near dark alleys
where one can get mugged). It will mean living wherever
one chooses. It will mean having maximum personal and
recreational choice. We can already see what it will look
like in the United States, because the most affluent are
already living it. (Farmer's Law—if you want to know
what people will be doing in twenty-five years, see what
the top 5 percent of income earners are doing now. They
are the group everyone emulates. In twenty-five years,
the average family income will be about what the top 5
percent is now, and they will be doing what the elite is
doing now. And what the elite is doing is moving to
lower-density living styles.)

In other words, look around and see what's selling
these days—the real world, the one you don't have to
plan or subsidize, is already taking shape, and it's happening very fast everywhere. And people are living this
way because they happen to want to, not because anyone
is making them. As I said, my vision of the future stems
from a very simple premise, namely that most people are
pretty smart, and they tend to do what is quite logical for
them. They also tend to maximize whatever they perceive to be freedom—which is sometimes not exactly
what others see it to be.

# 3

■ ■

# *The Death of the Cities*

Paul Smith had come home, after thirty-two years, and of course he went to church the first thing. He had grown up in Central City, gone to high school there, and left for good in 1940, when he started college. There was World War II, a continued college education thereafter, and business and engineering assignments all around the world after that. His parents had moved away, and there was really no reason to come home, but he finally had made it. So here he was, sitting in the richly Gothic Presbyterian downtown church he had attended as a boy, thinking through the sermon about what had happened even in his short lifetime. One obvious thing had occurred. The church was almost empty. He counted eighteen other worshipers besides himself, all of whom were very old. At fifty-one, he was obviously the youngest person there by at least ten years. It was almost spooky to sit in a huge, empty church, listening to an earnest old minister preach familiar precepts once again.

Central City was perhaps a typical middle-American place, with 250,000 people in the city, plus another 500,-000 scattered around the metropolitan area. Paul had noticed driving in from the airport the suburban explosion. There were houses where he had once hunted rabbits, and shopping centers seemed to be everywhere. Out on the freeway, new plants, offices, and two-story apartments had sprung up everywhere. Out there in suburbia, it was clear that business was good, things were picking up, and people were obviously much more affluent than they ever had been.

Downtown, in the middle of the central business district, it was different, a lot different. Paul had walked before church, looking around. There had been seven major movie theaters where he had often taken his girls for dates; now one was pretty seedy, another showed X-rated movies only, and still another was a revival temple. Four were deserted and empty. The big department store, where everyone who was anyone had shopped, stood empty, as did two of the three major hotels. Instead of the posh shops he remembered from his youth, he found only trinket operations, ticky-tacky kinds of souvenir joints, book stores with painted-over windows advertising sex magazines, and little short-order eating places. Paul found it easy to get around—nothing much was different, and all the big 1940 downtown buildings were still there.

Something had changed, though. The two big banks had built huge modern office buildings. There were a shiny new library and city hall, and the federal government also had built a nice new office building. All had plenty of parking around them, and they all seemed to be doing well, if the address lists in the lobbies were any indication. Paul realized that something else had happened too. A lot of buildings, particularly the old two-story brick jobs, weren't there any more. Instead, they were parking lots. Paul could remember that in 1940 you could never find a place to park downtown, because there was no parking space to speak of. So most people rode the long-gone streetcars. Well, he thought, time changes all things.

The service ended, and Paul stopped to chat with the minister. Yes, the church had lost a lot of members, and the reverend was concerned about it. In 1940, the church had drawn its membership from the solid citizens who lived along the old streetcar routes, who came in each Sunday. And the really prosperous burghers who had so richly endowed the church and kept it afloat even now, had lived in sumptuous mansions at the edge of the central city. The minister noted that the mansions were still there, boardinghouses where poor blacks lived. Our black brothers were of course welcome to the church, but most of them seemed to be Baptists, not Presbyterians, and unfortunately, too many of them didn't seem to go to church at all. Besides, many older parishioners felt nervous about coming downtown, even on a Sunday morning. Crime rates were way up and many thought that it was dangerous to be anywhere in town. Younger people went to church, if they did at all, in one of the four or five Presbyterian churches that had been built in recent years in the suburbs. It was easier, and of course such churches were neighborhood operations, where you knew the parishioners. The old minister was troubled by the change. He had been at this church since 1941—indeed, he had succeeded Paul's old minister when he retired, and everything seemed to be going downhill. The world and the city were not the same as they once had been.

After church, Paul walked around some more. He passed rather quickly out of the central-city core, out to the big brick warehouses and factories along the tracks. There was Bilger's, where he had worked one summer— it was abandoned and rotting. Actually, over half the buildings were abandoned, and Paul's engineering eye could quickly see that the ones in use were marginal. A few furniture warehouses, some other minor storage, and nothing else. Paul realized the city was dying. He could look up, over the downtown stores, and see the vacant space above them. Back in 1940, those offices had been full of dentists and lawyers, or even some little light manufacturing operation, like sewing shirts or making toys. Now there was nothing.

But as Paul moved on, there was plenty. The old residential areas were still lively enough—and all black. Paul felt awkward as he felt the stares of little black kids. He saw a wino drooped in a gutter, and he noticed the well-dressed people coming out of the shabby revivalist church which used to be solidly Methodist and all white. He was a stranger in his own land, and while he had been a stranger often before in distant countries, it was bothersome to find that he knew no one here.

Paul drifted back to his car downtown. There were parking meters all over, which didn't apply on Sunday. It figured—his was the only car parked on the whole block. He drove around a bit, finding that he could have safely shot a cannon down any street. Downtown was totally deserted. Paul started back up one of the main streets, along an old streetcar track, feeling strange. This city was not dying, it was dead already. Back in 1940, on any Sunday downtown would be packed with people going to the show, walking around, strolling in the parks, having a leisurely day. Now, nothing, nothing at all, except a black ghetto at the fringes, an idly cruising police car, and a few old folks coming home from church. You used to be able to get a streetcar, with a five-minute wait at most, after church. As Paul drove away, he noted that a couple of little old ladies had just got on an almost empty bus, over a half hour after church had let out. The town simply reeked of decay and death. Two or three more years, he realized, and he would have been the only one in church—if it still existed.

Paul drove to his motel along the freeway, where he was staying because he could easily park his car there. He picked up the local paper and read it. The city was in desperate financial trouble—the school budget was so far out of balance that school days would have to be cut sharply, and the voters had just rejected both a new bond issue and a property-tax hike. The mayor was hopeful that he could get some new federal money, but the reporter pointed out that even modest help from that source was unlikely for more than a year. The bus company, now a city operation, was four million in the red, and further cutbacks in service were threatened if a bigger government appropriation were not made. The police were threatening a strike, since their pay had not been raised in four years, and some residents had dumped a load of uncollected garbage on the mayor's lawn to protest the lousy service they were getting.

Paul felt that his initial reactions were justified. The cost of everything seemed to be going up, yet the tax base was obviously going down. Crime was up, decay was up, unemployment was up, people were bailing out, and things were in a big mess. And no one seemed to have any idea what to do, except ask Washington for some more cash. Even the city librarian was screaming because her budget had been cut 30 percent. The newspaper reporter noted acidly that book circulation out of the central library had fallen over 60 percent in the last twenty years, while costs had tripled. The schools still had lots of kids, mainly black, and they needed more help than an unused library.

Paul lay back on his bed, suddenly feeling very old. Where had the dreams gone? He remembered back to 1939, when he wrote a paper for his high school civics class. There was a war in Europe then, and it looked as if the country would finally get out of that endless depression that had stopped everything for over ten years. (The newest downtown building had been finished in 1930, and no one was starting any building in the 1930s.) The city would boom. Paul himself had gone to that old central library, looked up the data, talked to some Chamber of Commerce types. The city would have a million people by 1960, compared to 225,000 now, just wait and see! The men showed Paul their own sketches and dreams—huge high-rise apartments near town, new theaters downtown, new factories along the tracks near the city center, a new city hall, new parks, new everything. Just wait a few years, boy, and when you come back, you won't recognize the place! Central City is going to grow!

It sure as hell grew, Paul mused, but not quite the way they figured it would. They thought that it would grow up, way up, with high-rise buildings and elevators and a new rapid transit system. Instead, it grew out laterally, across the midwestern cornfields, way out beyond where the city had been, leaving a rotting core in the mighty city. Instead of great buildings rising off the plain, all you got were some suburban split-levels fourteen miles out of town. Not exactly what he used to think a great city was. What had happened? Paul remembered the lively growing European cities he had seen, the sort of inside-out cities in poorer countries, where the very poor live in shacks way out where American suburbs are, while the middle class lived in nice downtown apartments where American inner-city ghettos are. Something was funny about Central City—now what was it?

Paul was a logical man, an engineer and a manager, so he got out a sheet of motel stationary and jotted down what he thought:

Mistaken Premise 1: Cities have many functions. Virtually everyone who is concerned about cities these days assumes that cities have many functions. They did have once. Now they do not. Only four of the historically important functions remain, one of which is likely to disappear within ten years, thus affecting another. In the past fifty years, three major technological developments have wiped out the others. First, the automobile and the truck have led to a diffuse, land-extensive pattern of life, both residentially and commercially. Second, steam-motive power has been displaced by electricity, which also disperses activities. Third, the revolution in communications, most notably in telephones, leased lines, and television, likewise tends to disperse people. The following are those functions which are declining or lost:

1. Transport transfers. Most American cities initially were a terminal point for transport transfers, typically between rail and water. Hence there was a need for docks, labor to shift cargoes, and so forth. There also was a tendency to put many manufacturing facilities right at the transfer point, since this was an economical and logical location.

Much of this function now has been lost to motor trucks and airports. What processes remain are capital intensive (for example, containerization), and manpower needs are no longer as large, even where the function remains; these needs will become less manpower-oriented in the future. In addition, much of the transfer function has been lost to new transfer points, typically those highly specialized, at some outlying point. The rapid increase in ship size has meant that nineteenth-century docks and facilities are too small. Thus, when grains, oils, coal, or similar bulk items are transshipped, the process occurs in automated, highly land-extensive modern facilities out of town.

2. Manufacturing. Electricity and other modern technical developments have meant the removal of factories from the city to the suburbs, where low-lying, land-

extensive plants can function better. This phenomenon is closely related to the truck and automobile. Trucks can handle the loads more easily on wider roads designed for them; automobiles can carry the affluent, skilled workers to and from the scattered plants. This development is related directly to point 1, since these modern plants normally do not need to be exactly at the interchange point. Besides, older cities are not well designed for modern interchange from road to rail or vice versa; trucks were far in the future when most of our ports were laid out.

Moreover, much light manufacturing historically done near the city core is now done overseas. We import items once manufactured by the underpaid, unskilled persons who lived in our inner cities. An additional problem is that as larger firms move out to the suburbs many smaller service operations follow them. Tool-and-die shops, typewriter-repair operations, machine shops, and a host of other small enterprises now are located near the freeway.

3. Railroads. Railroads used to employ many men in operations, sorting, maintenance, and passenger activities. The passengers have migrated to the airports out of town; the diesel has revolutionized railroad repair work (there is much less of it); and the general decline of railroads has not helped (there are now 590,000 rail workers as compared to 1.5 million in 1945). Many passenger terminals and freight yards still clutter the city, but most are idle.

4. Warehousing. The warehousing function has followed the trucks and factories to the suburbs. With so many hauls now handled by trucks, and with automatic handling equipment so economical, it pays to have a single-story, land-extensive unit, like most modern warehouses. Note also the decreased use of unskilled labor to pack, sort, and stack, coupled with the use of more

skilled men to run lift trucks and operate computers. These skilled men now live in the suburbs and drive to work in their own cars.

5. Retailing. Much, although not all, retailing has followed the affluent customers, as retailing always does. Retail shops go where the people are, particularly those with money, and they are no longer in the city.

6. Entertainment. Television is the culprit, at least as far as mass entertainment is concerned. Those of us over forty can remember going downtown to the movies, but those days are gone. All that is left of this function are honky-tonks, sex movies, and other pitiful remnants. Gone with the movie places are the restaurants and short-order cafes that catered to the amusement crowd. Many kinds of entertainment and amusement facilities have followed their customers. Modern stadiums must have acres of parking, and most successful restaurants are in the suburbs near affluent customers.

7. High-level services. Doctors, dentists, and optometrists are likely to be found in the suburbs also, near their paying patients.

8. Wholesaling. Like warehousing, wholesaling has gone in search of extensive land for low-lying storage.

9. Conventions and other meetings. As the rest of the central city decays, it becomes more and more attractive to hold meetings at the newer locations such as airports and suburban hotels or motels. There are still many big conventions downtown, but the shift is apparent, and undoubtedly will accelerate. It is also easier to take an airplane to some exotic resort, and it will get easier still.

All these functions once provided employment and income for city dwellers, both directly and indirectly. Vestigial remains still can be found in any American city, but they are dying, and as they die we witness the now familiar pattern. The affluent move away, following or attracting the jobs and services they need. The old houses, placed near economic activities for the convenience of persons without cars, remain, but the transport system and the economic functions have disappeared. The modern forces of electricity, motor vehicles, and communication are all dispersive forces, yet we seem sometimes to think that we can restore our old cities without the basic functions which made them useful in the first place.

The following include those functions which remain in the cities:

1. Brokering. The term "brokering" is shorthand for the various things people do which require face-to-face contact. Professional buying and selling, negotiating contracts, consulting, much legal work, and many related activities where men like to see each other as they work. This explains why office buildings are the only successful recent additions in many cities.

2. Government. Local, state, and federal governments are very active. Because they insist on being downtown, many related activities must occur there. This point also relates to point 1, since many face-to-face problems involve public organizations and government. Actually, many government activities could take place more efficiently elsewhere, but government, more than any other organization, has tried to keep people in the city.

3. Housing for poor people. Cities are full of obsolete housing as a result of their decline. Since the affluent do not choose to live in such places, those who do tend to be poor. Of course, they have far fewer employment opportunities than those who once lived there, since the functions of the city have disappeared. They also cannot always afford cars so their mobility is limited.

4. Petty retail and service activities for what's left. We still need luncheon counters, retail shops, and so forth for the remaining functions. These tend to be high-cost, inefficient operations because they have to be located in

high-cost, inefficient buildings. Supermarkets and shopping centers, built with the automobile and truck in mind, are more efficient.

In the future it may satisfy businessmen and administrators to watch each other on a TV telephone as they talk. If so, this and similar electronic devices will make it less attractive to be where people are, in other words in the city. Who wants to go downtown when everything essential can be done in a quiet, pleasant suburban office? With the withdrawal of brokering will come the further decline of service establishments to serve the vanished brokers.

Mistaken Premise 2: People like to live under crowded conditions. There is a great deal of evidence that most of them do not. After all, in the past forty years millions of persons have fled cities as fast as their incomes permitted. A certain return to congestion in recent years, indicated by the sharp increase in apartment building at the expense of single-unit homes, is more indicative of defects in home financing than of actual personal desires.

A few persons (perhaps 20 percent of the population) do like living in populated areas. These include mainly young people, who like the excitement, and many older people, who prefer to be able to walk to stores and other facilities. The majority obviously want to be where they can grow a bit, stretch a bit, and park their cars. Given most modern life styles, this is a perfectly reasonable way to live, and most are doing so or are trying to. Housing solutions which exclude the automobile (including any plans to push people into congested, high-rise areas) are not likely to work well.

Mistaken Premise 3: Restoring 1910-style rapid transit (even with modern comfortable seats and air conditioning) will somehow make us all go back downtown. Those who will use such systems would use them regardless, namely the very poor (returning to the inner city from jobs outside of town), businessmen with offices downtown, and government employees. Given that most other functions are elsewhere, why should anyone else go to the inner city?

Rapid transit needs large volumes of people at each end of the line. The typical suburb is not high-density, nor do people living there travel downtown very often. As a result, we can confidently predict that if billions of public dollars are spent on transport systems, few will use them, and those few will not enjoy it.

Mistaken Premise 4: Tearing down and rebuilding the traditional city will somehow restore it. Given the flight of functions from the city, nothing that is now being done is likely to bring many people back. It is nonsense to assume that restoring modest entertainment functions in addition to government offices will somehow revitalize the city.

The main reason most cities have managed to do as well as they have is because a large part of them has been torn down, not so much by urban renewal projects as by private entrepreneurs who removed many marginal buildings to create parking lots. Without this development the cities would have had many more problems than they do. Streetcar cities are not adaptable to the automobile and truck, and no amount of restructuring will change this fundamental fact.

Mistaken Premise 5: People are nice guys. The modern American assumption, particularly in social work and government, is that we are all equal and nice. Programs designed to improve anyone or anything are designed to operate by persuasion; threats are brutal, degrading, and passé. This premise is typically incorrect where the poor are concerned, because, like the poor everywhere (including our own ancestors), they cannot afford to be very nice; they are too busy eking out a living. Our cities increasingly are dealing with the very poor. Since the poor are rarely nice guys, solutions that seem sound rarely work well in the inner city. We expect the poor, for example, to pick up their garbage, keep the neighborhood clean, and stay in school because nice people do; they do not and will not.

The premise also precludes any system of threats, which might get results, or any reward system based on performance. We are going to have threat systems whether we like it or not (for example, police power), and without reward systems we cannot encourage people to do the right things, regardless of whether or not they want to. Instead, our operations are based on being nice to people. Ethically, this is clearly desirable—unless the systems break down, which is exactly what is happening.

Mistaken Premise 6: Sunk costs are relevant. The first principle an economist learns is that historic costs, expenses incurred in the past, should not be used when making current decisions. The reason is simple: you will often fail to take advantage of present potential. This is particularly unfortunate if those present possibilities involve abandoning something that once seemed useful. Few people are economists, however, and the vestiges of our Calvinistic consciences impels us to save string, turn out lights, and try to use, somehow, the billions invested in streets, power systems, gas and water mains, housing, and so forth. Usually these things are not really useful, and the mistaken assumption that they should be used makes our decisions about the city wrong. Of course, the owners of all those assets, who desperately are trying to salvage what they can, apply lots of pressure on the decision makers. We cannot blame them, but neither do we have to listen to them.

Paul stopped, reread his notes, and crumbled them up and tossed them in the wastebasket. Hell, he thought, there's no way an old-fashioned city could survive into the 1980s. He went down to the bar, had a drink, and tried to forget about what might have been, if cars and telephones and television and other things hadn't come along, and if he had stayed in the city the way he always thought he would when he and the world were young.

# 4

## Two Urban Tomorrows

Our cities won't disappear by 1984, or even 2004. A lot of people will still be struggling with them, and a lot of obsolete real estate will still exist, in or out of use. And a lot of existing political entities, like central-city governments, will still have massive problems. Many middle- and upper-middle-class Americans will have forgotten them, but society cannot. What do we do?

Percolating along in the American political economy are two possible tomorrows for the city. Each has already shown some life; each is considerably different from the other, and each would have quite different results. Suppose, instead of agonizing about all the problems cities now have, we got smart about some presently feasible solutions. Suppose we actually found the political wisdom to begin to apply them, and we adapted the city of the future to what people really want. Let's take a trip through Central City, 1984, the way it just might be. . . .

You approach the city driving in along the freeway, just as you now do. But your car is running on hydrogen, instead of gasoline. Since burned hydrogen becomes water, your car is a totally nonpolluting vehicle. The scientists and technicians had a devil of a job getting the system right—hydrogen gas is quite explosive, and getting enough hydrogen from water to begin with also created some real problems—but your car is new and it works fine. Plenty of 1975 gasoline-powered cars are still around, but there are fewer of them each year. Already the air is noticeably cleaner.

Your car radio announces that for the ninth straight year, the pollution index has dropped. All that work on antipollution has begun to pay off, and the very rapid increases in the price of oil, coal, and natural gas in the early 1970s encouraged lots of research on other, nonpolluting power sources. Now your city has much more atomic power than anyone expected in 1973. Many of the newer homes are also using hydrogen gas since natural gas has become quite scarce, and more families are switching over every day.

Industrial firms are under very tight pollution controls, as they have been for a decade or more. And many of them, to their surprise, have found that it pays—what they retrieved from smokestacks and water discharges turned out to contain all sorts of reusable chemicals and metals, such as sulphur and silver, which can be sold for good prices in rising markets. Remember that every decade it is a bit harder to find and extract virgin metal deposits.

You get off the freeway twenty miles out of town, onto a local road. All around you, widely scattered, are eighty-thousand-dollar houses that clearly were not built out of farming profits on this marginal, rocky land. People are still moving out from the city to five acres and the memory of a farm. They commute into town, or more commonly work at home, using their video telephones and

cable systems to stay in touch with the home office. Ironi-
cally, the Rural Electrification Administration, which was
set up in the 1930s to bring farmers the benefits of electricity, now serves mainly the upper middle class. String-
ing all those electric lines around the countryside made
those high-priced homes possible.

Closer to the city, you begin to encounter the suburbs
of 1973. The lawns are trimmed and neat, and fresh
paint is everywhere. Houses last a long, long time, particularly if they are desirable. There are some more
shopping centers, with lots of parking around them, and
a few consolidated schools, with yellow buses to bring in
the exurban kids from the homes you saw still further
out. A few old farms are now parks, and there are some
new factories strung out along the freeways, but otherwise, this area could be 1973 all over again. It figures—
this part of the metropolitan area was built the way people wanted it, so it has stayed pretty much the same.

As you get still closer in, you see lots more low rise,
two-story apartments, laid out in *U* shapes, with swimming pools and lots of parking. Some carry ads for old
people; others, near new schools, encourage children;
still others catering to singles state that no children are
allowed. The parkland, swimming pools, and golf
courses around these are clearly for adult tastes. Indeed,
if you look closely, you will see many fewer children than
in 1973—the birthrate has been dropping, and the government is even beginning to be concerned. You could
have seen a very similar scene in West Los Angeles or
Oak Park in 1965. The low-lying apartment houses are
new, but they are very similar to units built years ago.
There are just more of them.

As you drive into downtown, you note that even
though this is the morning rush hour, there are fewer
cars than you remembered, and more people are in each
car. Lots of people are working at home, while many

others are driving away from town, since their work is in a suburban office or factory. You turn on your radio, and a fellow is advertising the local "find a buddy" system. Send in your address, place of work, travel times, and two dollars, and in a few days the computer will send you a list of fifty people who live within a mile of you, and who have the same travel pattern you have. You can then find any of them you want for your car pool. Today you haven't got a passenger, and above you a sign flashes: SINGLES TO RIGHT LANE TO PAY TOLL 1/4 MILE. You pull over and wait—you wait quite a while, behind several other cars. An old fellow at the tollbooth is laboriously making change, and it takes him a long time. You realize that maybe there is method in this madness, as you watch the loaded cars zip by. After all, what is scarce in a potentially congested highway is street space, and a car with three or four passengers in it is using a lot less freeway space per passenger than you are. The longer it takes you to get through the tollgate, the more likely it will be that next time you will find a couple of passengers. The effect is to reduce the number of cars using crowded streets and freeways during rush hours. Fewer cars handle the same number of people.

It is easy to see why very few new freeways have had to be built. Instead of following the old pattern of building more roads whenever congestion appeared, regardless of the cost or what it did to neighborhoods or raw land, the government now uses its existing roads better. Back in 1974 there was an average of only 1.3 persons in each car during the rush hour. Now, with 2.5 people per car, and much more diffusion of economic and social activities, congestion has pretty much disappeared. Incidentally, it's also true that the population has not increased, and in 1973 most families who wanted cars already had them.

As you drop off the freeway onto an inner-city street,

the most striking feature is how uncrowded things are. Instead of moldering flats built in 1910, there are goodly numbers of open lots. Ancient warehouses, long abandoned or turned to very marginal uses, are gone, replaced here and there by low-rise two-story apartments like the ones you just saw. The air is a lot cleaner too—the acrid smog you remember is gone. There are still some older houses, often lots of them, standing proud and firm as they did when they were built in 1910 or 1913. In the old days, these houses were wall to wall, block after block. But someone has weeded out three or four houses on each block, sometimes a few more. And those empty areas are either paved for parking, or planted with grass, so the kids can play. Miniparks, really, a bit of free space.

You watch one of the old houses being rebuilt. The contractor is tearing out the old wiring and plumbing, and putting in new stuff—clearly not a job being paid for by some illiterate inner-city poor person. Down the street, an obviously affluent couple are doing their own painting on their 1910 masterpiece, which is all alive again with its fine old woods and leaded glass windows. A brief chat confirms that the young man just bought this wreck from the city at a good price, considering all the work that needed to be done. He and his wife used to live in one of those singles apartments, but they wanted a house of their own. Since the classical suburban split-level turned them off, when they heard about this old house, and for half the price of a new one, they bought it. When they finished working on it, it would more than double in value. Of course, they couldn't have done this even a few years ago, since there would have been no place to park their car. Now, with the new space two doors down where an old deserted house had been raised, plus the small playground near the corner, the house met every need they had.

The young man takes you in to show you what he's done. Amid the painting rags and other confusion, you can see the fine wood in the staircase, the magnificent molding work, the huge, ancient fireplace that will be working pretty soon, once the chimney gets cleaned. The owner will probably have to do it himself, but do it he will. You think back about the bulldozers only ten years back, leveling hundreds of such fine old houses in your city to build high-rise apartments, and wonder why someone didn't think about making some off the street parking where none existed before. People have been giving up everything, including fine old houses, for cars for fifty years—it seems much more sensible to make some room for the cars, save what's left.

When the program of weeding out a few old houses in each block first started in 1976 in Central City, the citizens worried about forcing the poor into the street. A quick investigation showed that many old houses were actually empty. The poor blacks who had lived in them had long since moved on to better housing in the gilded ghetto. Indeed, the city was found to own large numbers of these older houses. It bulldozed down a few here and there, paving over the available space or planting grass and trees. At the same time, the federal government restructured a few housing finance programs, focusing them on the buyer, not on the neighborhood. In 1973, an affluent buyer trying to finance a very old house in the inner city would find that many areas were blacklisted for such loans. But the new program simply assumes that a family with income that wants to move into a dump must know what it's doing. A few smart (and now fast-growing) local banks spotted this trend and began to provide mortgage money. Now the whole area was going up in value again—land and houses were at a premium—and tax revenues were actually higher than they had been when poor families huddled in the older houses because they had no place else to go. The area had been subtly adjusted to the automobile, it was beginning to come alive once again.

You're puzzled where the poor went, so you drive around some more. They are there, but less visibly since there are fewer of them. Incomes have steadily risen, and while there is still a bottom 10 percent, they are more affluent than the 1973 bottom 10 percent. They are also dispersed. Some bright guy figured out that the poor like space just like anyone else. They also like to be near whatever jobs are around. So as you drive about looking, you see an occasional low-rise apartment, with some poor people in it. You also see an occasional mobile home, stuck way back on some cleared lot or another, and you remember that back in the suburbs you caught a glimpse of an occasional house trailer way back in the trees, even in affluent neighborhoods. It seems the government found out something interesting. While anyone will scream if someone suggests housing the poor in a thirty-five-story high rise right next door, practically no one gets up tight about one mobile home, not even one put in the woods near upper-income housing. A very smart welfare agency got a mother with three kids to live in it, and the lady was willing and eager to work. The upper-income housewives got a servant, caterer, and cleaning woman; the woman's kids got into one of the best suburban schools around. And there was only one such family in the whole school district. Apparently almost anyone can survive three or four smiling black faces out of three hundred.

You do some arithmetic. Of the blacks living here in 1973, a third were already middle-class. Another third were sober, reliable blue-collar types, with jobs, hoping for a future for their kids. The last third, down in the inner city, were the hard-core problem. In the decade gone by, quite a few of those hard-core have either died (many were older, uneducated people), or learned skills and got jobs, or grew up and locked into the mainstream world. When you get right down to it, the numbers to get out of the ghetto are not really all that big—so, off to mobile homes, an occasional small suburban house here and there, or a low-rise apartment someplace else. And suddenly the ghetto is very empty.

As you drive around the inner-city core, the cruddy old warehouses, in very marginal use in 1973, are all gone, as are the moldering 1920 six-story apartments, ancient factories, and even railroad yards. It seems that some years back Central City finally voted in a land tax. Of course, this radical legislation was violently fought by real estate speculators, but it got through. Property owners began to pay taxes based on what the land *should* be used for, not what it *was* used for. The buildings and improvements were not taxed at all.

Under the old rules, as your property deteriorated, your taxes went down, since the buildings were worth less every year. Any half-witted speculator could sit on a moldering warehouse near the city center, waiting to see if the government would want his land for some grandiose new development. He could afford to wait, since his taxes were modest. Or he could tear down his building and make a parking lot. Without the building, taxes were cheaper still, and the landlord could make some money waiting for the hoped-for price increase. Slumlords let their properties deteriorate, since if they improved their property, their taxes would rise.

Under the new tax rules, an ancient warehouse on land which really should be used for low-rise apartments, is taxed as if those modern apartments were on it. A tax bill for perhaps five thousand dollars becomes a bill for eighteen thousand. Holding idle or misused land gets very expensive. So what happened was some owners sold out to developers who used the land right; other owners decided to develop it themselves. Still others abandoned their land to the city for taxes. The city then promptly bulldozed down the old warehouse and planted trees. And rather quickly the inner city became a place where land was used right. Incidentally, that young couple rebuilding their old house paid the property tax for a modest single-family house which was indeed on the property. But as they improved their home, they did not face higher taxes. In effect, the more they fixed it up the more valuable the house got, and the lower their tax burden was per unit of investment. The city was rewarding them, not punishing them for their part in making the city livable again.

As you look around, you also notice that everything is a lot cleaner. Some poor kids are busily picking up garbage. *Kids, picking up trash?* Some behavioral scientist must have invented a mind-bending drug. A short talk with the boys and girls suggests what's up. A trash truck is going to come around shortly, and if the kids fill it, they get paid. Somewhere along the line the city fathers got smart and began to pay for results. And they got them! Why keep running uphill, with big organizations trying to do things no one wanted to do anyhow, like pick up trash and garbage? Why not just pay anyone who would do these things? Cash on the line, no questions asked. It turned out to be a lot cheaper than welfare, to say nothing of those administrative overheads.

A bit further along, you find yourself in what seems to be an old, respectable, 1935 neighborhood. The houses are in very good shape, well painted and maintained. Why not, with all those bonuses to their owners for keeping them up? You see lots of smiling black faces, little children that look so clean that they seem polished, playing on their neat, well-trimmed lawns. You're in the gilded ghetto.

By 1984, it will be much easier for blacks to move out of Central City like the rest of us, and many of them, particularly the younger people, who got a good education, will. But lots of people still like to be with their own kind, however they define that. Hence lots of blacks may well want to live near other blacks. These minorities want all the freedom instruments, and a good 1935 house can provide them—if the parking is there, and if the wiring is rebuilt to handle heavy modern electrical loads. You note that the houses all have garages.

Farther down toward the center of town, you see a familiar sight, the old midtown university. The 1878 buildings are still there, along with some new ones. Since some of the old houses around the neighborhood have been weeded out and all of the warehouses and factories demolished, you can see the place the way it must have looked when it was first built, surrounded again by a low-density living pattern. The houses that remain are the 1890 professors' mansions. A quick price check shows you that unless you're rich, you can't afford to live here—after all, living near a nice place like a good university has always been desirable. Now, with some of the older homes restored to their original elegance, and with some parking places and parkland around them, they are still desirable.

You note that the road network near the university is a bit better, too—a few ancient streets have been straightened out, and the 1974 freeway is not so far away. You have stumbled on a city node, a place where people still gather together to accomplish something. But instead of fighting downtown to get there, then fearing for your life in a slum surrounding the place, you now find the whole neighborhood a pleasure to get to and be in. There is another university way out at the edge of the suburban area too, and it is another node, built in 1978. This one might have been abandoned but all it took to bring it back was some horse sense about using the land around it.

Later on, you'll find more nodes in the city—the hospital and medical research complex, the stadium and sports center, the natural history museum, the art gallery, the performing theater, and the government center. Some of these nodes, like the stadium, will be out in the old suburbia. Others will be almost in the old downtown, now restructured to resemble in form and function those newer suburban ones. All of these nodes have one major characteristic in common—they can be easily reached by car. And this also means that they will not be in high-density neighborhoods. For a long time, cities tried to save themselves by increasing density, and it didn't work. Now, accepting the inevitable, they are beginning to become a new kind of lower density. In the process they have become viable again. A lot of the desirable older buildings, parks, museums, and other attractions have become lovely and useful again, instead of rotting with all the undesirable stuff.

As you drive on, you realize there has to be a really crummy, high-crime, old-fashioned ghetto around someplace. So you go looking, and you find it—it's small, but it's still there. The winos drowse in the gutters; the houses are falling apart; store front revivalist churches urge you to repent; and little mama-papa cigar stores and groceries hide behind mesh protective grills. But you're listening to the radio as you drive, and the announcer reports that crime rates are down for the ninth straight year. Why? The answer is lowering population densities tends to lower crime rates, particularly personal crimes like mugging, which require that the criminal find his victim. And historically many crimes are committed by young people, of whom there are many fewer in 1984. And the state has legalized crimes against one's self, such as drunkenness and petty gambling.

Now how do people get around? After all, the pensioners and school children still need transportation. A bit of investigation shows you how it's done. There are plenty of taxis around, and the fares they charge are actually lower than you remember. Why? The city got smart and licensed lots of new owners. Until 1976, there had been no new taxi operators in the city since 1931. The business was a cartel—with high prices, lousy service, and careful controls to protect the operators, not the riders. Now they let anyone in, provided he can drive and has insurance. With higher personal incomes and lower taxi fares, lots of old ladies can afford the trip. Moreover, you keep seeing JITNEY signs on lots of cars and vans. A jitney is a car used like a bus—it drives any route, picks up enough passengers to fill up, and drives directly to its destination. Poor countries, like Lebanon and the Philippines, have had them for decades. They are cheap, fast, and convenient. Before 1925, they were outlawed in most American cities to protect the streetcars. When the streetcars disappeared, the laws against jitneys remained and no one remembered how convenient they had been.

Jitneys and taxis fit the 1984 city well, since they can go just about anywhere with very few people. Rapid transit lines and buses run in straight lines to and from downtown. Since the 1984 low-rise city is all over the place, with no big traffic along any single route, Central City provides the transport people can use. Hustling taxis and jitneys flow around in all directions, and they don't cost the city a cent. Private businessmen are doing it all, and making a few bucks besides. For the ill, the desperately poor, and the lame, the city does have cars with two-way radios to help out. Their drivers take old men to and from the hospital; charity cases to visit relatives; and oldsters to shop.

When you come to the heart of downtown, it looks the same at first glance: big high-rise office buildings, banks, and government buildings. But when you look closely, you can see that downtown is just another node, where some few people find it convenient to work. In spite of

TV telephones, on-line computers, and other electronic communications, it is sometimes useful to get together to talk—and downtown is structured to make this easy. There is much more parking space, the street network is improved, and it is cleaner than it used to be. As you park your car and go about your business, you decide that Central City has come a long, long way.

This new type of exurban city bothers planners. It looks bad from the overall point of view. Planners see things on a cosmic scale, and those scale models of the developments they want to build are evidence of this. What looks good, impressive, lively, and dramatic in a scale model, seen as if the viewer were in an airplane above it, are high-rise buildings, massively concentrated facilities, and huge amphitheaters thrusting themselves into the landscape. What is so exciting about local neighborhoods, a few activity nodes here and there, and long stretches of single family homes, small apartments, and open space? There is no overall rhyme or reason. Why, it even begins to look like Los Angeles! But from the personal point of view, when the five-and-a-half-foot human finally walks around way down there in the huge development, the whole thing is frightening and distasteful. The typical homeowner, who parks his car down the street, who watches his kids play on the grass, and who sits on his back porch actually sees only a very little piece of the total. And what he selects to see is pleasant to him and his family. A 50-by-100-foot minipark, a similar-sized parking lot, plus an older, yet very attractive house, looks good to the individual. It's the kind of neighborhood people like to walk in, even to work in. If the scene is repeated across ten miles of similar miniblocks, he doesn't care. After all, he will only live in one of them, work in another, and have relatives or friends in a few more. What seems horribly monotonous to the over-viewer actually is very diverse and interesting to the man down there living in it. And in this 1984 city, there actually *is* diversity. Some of the blocks and neighborhoods are very old; some are brand-new; others are mixes of the old and new; some are grouped around shopping centers; some around educational institutions; some around employment opportunities or sporting facilities. Whatever the individual and his family want they find for themselves, leaving other people to find whatever they want—whatever that happens to be.

So there is one city of tomorrow. It's no utopia, but it makes the most of what we've got. It is not a matter of money or talent, but simply recognizing that the historic city is gone for good. It is seeing that it is easier to work with the times than against them. It could happen if we have the guts and imagination, and develop the detailed knowledge to pull it off. How much would it cost to build Central City 1984? Not any more than our present reconstruction plans, and probably a lot less. Buying and demolishing old buildings may seem expensive, until one realizes that the cities already own many abandoned inner-city buildings anyhow. The cost of just one rapid transit line, which probably won't work, might be a billion dollars or more for one modest-size city like Indianapolis or Cincinnati. That much money applied to the task of making cities livable on a human scale would do the entire job and leave half a billion to do something useful with.

The city in tomorrow number-two is the one we have plans to reconstruct. We plan to spend billions, with many more billions to come, to make it real. Fundamentally, it is a streetcar city which we believe is well worth having. The first obvious task is to revitalize urban transit which has virtually collapsed. Anyone who has waited for an hour or more for a bus can easily testify to that, and riding levels on urban transit systems are less than half what they were in 1945, in spite of huge population increases. Smaller cities will get brand-new hardware, like buses, which can be obtained cheaply and quickly. They will find, like those cities that have tried it, even with new air-conditioned buses and all the latest conveniences, that it doesn't work. People just don't like to ride them. Too few Americans who have money are willing to put up with the tyranny of bus schedules and the nonselective personal contact that riding buses implies. Moreover, buses take longer and often cost more.

So, how about rapid transit? The San Francisco Bay area has built a brand new system; Chicago has extended and upgraded its operation; Washington, D.C., has a modern system under construction; and Atlanta is now planning one. Unfortunately, it takes decades to build a really big, complex system—San Francisco started its construction in 1960, and operation of only one small part of the total system began in 1972. There is no hope for cities without mass transit facilities until the mid-1980s—which may be far too late. Rapid transit has other drawbacks. Cities that now have fast, fairly modern systems have lost traffic anyway. This really isn't too surprising, since these mass-flow, high-capacity systems run straight from the outlying high-density areas to downtown. Except in the rush hours, no one wants to get there from here. Thus, even as many cities clamor for federal funding for mass transit, Chicago loses $200 to $300 million a year on its fine, fast system, while cutting back operations. Smaller cities (from 500,000 to 2 million) find that the typical pattern is repeated with their buses. As traffic continues to fall, bus lines get cut back, and the private company begins to lose money. The city buys the line, gets some funding to buy new buses, and continues to operate at a loss. Citizens demand lower fares, and sometimes get them. Traffic goes up, but never as fast as the fare is cut, so the city hauls more people for less money at greater losses. At this point, some one discovers the subway train, and the call goes to Washington to fund a billion-dollar rapid transit project. No city in the United States has beaten this cycle, and even Toronto, the place which is supposed to be different, loses some $30 to $40 million a year on its streetcar, subway, and bus operations.

Despite the facts, the pressure for rapid transit is easy to understand. City officials, trapped by historic boundaries, have to optimize for the central city, which means rebuilding downtown. Property owners, who in most downtowns have seen front-foot values decline steadily since 1930 (!), know that if all those people will only come back, values will rise again. Since the transit line is being built with someone else's money, they support it. It is better than nothing. Construction companies and equipment suppliers, seeing those billion-dollar contracts, are ardent supporters of the new systems. And engineers who want to try out their new technologies like them too. But none of them give much thought to the inevitably public nature of the system, which violates those private freedoms so many Americans hold dear. A few taxpayers grumble, but they are scattered and diffuse. So public transit ends up being hailed as the savior of cities. And already we have federal programs, raids on the highway fund, and much interest in subway systems. This would be great if the systems worked, but we are going to be very disillusioned when they are built. People will ride them once or twice, yawn, and move out to the exurbs the way they always intended to.

The sad part is these new systems will be extremely expensive. A billion to two billion dollars is the commonly accepted cost for an adequate system to serve an urban area of from three to five million people. Since absolutely no one expects a rapid transit system to pay anything but its operating costs, the entire capital investment will be borne by the government. The government's hope is that there will be enough new-apartment and other high-rise construction along the line to increase real estate taxes enough to pay the bond interest. At tax-exempt city-bond rates (or the approximate interest cost on federal funds, if they are used), a billion-dollar system would cost taxpayers fifty million dollars in interest a year. For that kind of money, a personalized, chauffeur-driven car service could be provided for just about every carless person in the city.

Another part of our second tomorrow is the subsidized city: namely, getting the costs underwritten by the federal government. Cities want unrestricted revenue sharing; but the feds are more cautious, since they know very well that what local politicians want may only be useful to the politicians. Unrestricted revenue-sharing also gives control of funds to someone else. It is also true that when some funds have been given, the results are not exciting. When local police forces received unrestricted grants, they bought new toys, like airplanes, better two-way radios, nicer uniforms, and new guns. The connection between these expenditures and crime rates is tenuous.

There is another reason to doubt the efficacy of the subsidized city. Cities have productivity problems. Local government traditionally has had to provide labor intensive services, where productivity improvements are particularly difficult to get. Teachers continue to teach a class of thirty or so, even though wages rise; firemen perform the same services year after year, without much change in output per man; and sanitation departments also pay more to remove the same old garbage. The public pays more and more for less and less. Cities have no profit incentives, and the way local government is structured makes it easy to get pay up, improve working conditions and raise fringe benefits, without much pressure to improve performance. Civil service regulations don't help a reform-minded mayor either. In one major midwestern city, the new mayor can appoint only around twenty of the thousand city decision-makers. If the old guard doesn't like his pressure, they don't have to do a thing. The likely forecast is that unrestricted revenue-sharing will simply allow lots of cities to carry on costly and high-level services to a steadily diminishing population.

Another dimension of our second tomorrow is heavy investment in cities. Housing units for inner-city poor; downtown public and private buildings; sewer, electric, and water improvements; and urban renewal projects are a part of the package. The public buildings do get used, and the public housing does get lived in (although scandals are found everywhere), and anyone in the area who needs better utilities will happily use whatever gets built. Such expenditures do help somewhat. Jobs are created. The private sector helps out by financing what is still viable, like office buildings, which are a drop in the bucket compared to the needs. But so far, these improvements are a holding action, surrounded by lots of vacant ground which was once used for marginal buildings now torn down. Since the city has not got the functions it used to have, the suburban types are not coming back. In some places (e.g., St. Louis), the middle class still is getting out fast, and all kinds of apartment housing are in deep financial trouble.

Poverty programs are another attempt at city revitalization. Many agencies try to help out the urban poor, and dozens of public programs already are functioning. Coming down the road seems to be some form of income maintenance, meaning government just gives money to poor people. These programs work, in a slow but general way. Absolute levels of poverty have been eased in the past decade. But what do the newly affluent do? They get out too, even the blacks.

So where does this second tomorrow lead? To a

steadily depopulating inner city; some few activities in the center city, where a few buildings are put up; a new rapid transit system for upper-income commuters; a little new but fast-decaying housing in the ghetto for people who probably would just as soon be someplace else; and brand new buses running around almost empty. It's not an appealing picture. The fact is most Americans just don't want to live in the central city, the inner city, or anyplace else where population densities are high. Why should they? There is precious little to gain, and lots to lose.

Unfortunately, this second tomorrow is much more likely than our first, for several compelling reasons. But the real reason is emotional. We still think we want those high-rise cities, those 1910 crowds, those dramatic new buildings, whether we actually do or not. So we will end up with the tragedy of half-finished second-tomorrow cities that no one wants, while all the potential of a real twenty-first century city is wasted. Too bad!

## New York Is Different

In Manhattan Island, population densities are five to ten times higher per square mile than in any other city. There is no way to use cars in such a situation, so the island has to rely mainly on public transit. Someone once calculated that if every Manhattan commuter got a parking place, the whole island would be one big parking lot.

New York has this very high population density for several reasons. It was the first major success among nineteenth-century cities, largely because of its very desirable location, with all that water around it for cheap transport, plus its relatively central location between Boston and Washington. Where else in those days would you put your executive headquarters? For a century now,

New York City has been the financial, managerial, and executive center of the United States. The tight concentration of these functions gives Manhattan its special flavor. New York is also where it's at in entertainment, communications, publications, managerial consulting, high-powered law, finance, and many other highly skilled professions. This type of work, more than most, involves a great deal of face-to-face contact, which means using old-fashioned office complexes. This fact leads to very high population densities downtown during working hours.

Because Manhattan has such a high population density, it still has lots of highly specialized retail and service functions that most cities have now lost. If 1 percent of Manhattanites want or need something, then it will be provided, but if 1 percent of Denverites want it—well, would you believe a quick trip to New York City? Other American cities are just too diffuse, even in their most congested downtown areas, to have such high specialization. It is wishful thinking to hope that Cincinnati or Indianapolis will be competitive.

New York City is a very public place. You don't wash your clothes in your basement laundry room in New York, because you don't have a basement. So dirty clothes go out to the laundry, which is still active. You take the subway, since you can't feasibly own a car. You go to public entertainment such as live Broadway theater. And if you want to run some sort of European stall shop, or own a pushcart, you find your customers in New York City, not in Fort Wayne. In a way, New York is European, because with many fewer cars, telephones, and TV sets per capita, Europeans live this way too. You can also see a similiar phenomenon in Toronto, which had a half-million low-income European immigrants. Downtown Toronto is jumping all the time, just like Manhattan, since many citizens are still living the public life. It is also true that many Americans prefer the older, pre-auto life styles. If they do, they tend to self-select themselves into New York.

But even New York and Toronto are having their problems. The middle class is marching to the suburbs, and if those two-way TV telephones and other communications devices come in strong, much face-to-face contact won't be necessary any more. It is also true that high density means very high costs. You don't need multimillion-dollar elevator systems in a one-story office building, nor do you need the levels of police, fire, and social services you have to have in Manhattan. And as civic wage costs increase, taxes rise inexorably. It may be interesting and exciting to many, but it's a very expensive way of life. Therefore, some of the activities are already drifting out, and more are likely to follow. Only the poor actually stay in the city, since they have no options.

New York could have lots of tomorrows, depending on our political process and on how fast the new freedom instruments, like TV telephones, come into general use. One is that, given Manhattan's concentration of power and wealth, it can contrive to live off the federal dole. Corporate headquarters, stock markets, and banks will drift to the suburbs, or even farther out, but New York will be held together with public money from someplace else. Another possibility, deeply desired by many, is some sort of revitalization. Because this follows our second tomorrow, expect that plenty of public money will be spent on mass transportation, high-rise apartments, office buildings, and all the rest before anyone admits defeat. The most likely tomorrow is slow and steady decline, for a long, long time—like fifty years or more. There will be checkpoints as the years roll on—further withdrawal of the middle classes, rising vacancy rates in office buildings, apartments with rental problems, the flight of the minorities as they get some income and find better suburban homes, still more flight of light industry, more tax problems caused by building abandonments, and continuous labor troubles with the public unions as the city tries to save some money that it doesn't have. New York is so big it will take decades to get down to size.

Out in the low-density Midwest, when a company wants to send a young man to its Manhattan head office, it normally offers a hardship-post bonus of up to 25 percent of base salary. Nevertheless, so many married men with families refuse to go that many companies are having to think about getting out of New York. When the biggest, most interesting city in the country is ranked along with Afghanistan and Bolivia as a desirable place to be, one wonders. But the New York City of old haunts us, and we all are influenced by the dream. But it won't happen, not in 1984 or ever.

The cities of Europe will go exactly the same way, only it will take longer. In most West European countries, auto ownership per capita is not yet as high as it was in the United States in 1929. Land is much scarcer and more expensive, and upper-middle-class types are not about to let the peasants get out of cities without a struggle—remember European countries have much tougher class structures than we do. But wherever you go in Europe, if you drive out of town, you can see what's beginning to happen. The same single-family houses are being built as those near Philadelphia, and the same kinds of land use are coming in fast. By the year 2000, most of Western Europe will be talking about the same problems we Americans now debate. It could happen even sooner, if land-use planners take the position that such dispersal is useful.

Japan is also on the same road. Take the new high-speed train from Tokoyo to Osaka, and along the way you can see the new suburban streets marching across the rice paddies, with neat little single-family houses being built. It's actually happening even though Japan is way behind Europe, both in car ownership and land availability, to say nothing of sewers, streets, and highways.

Although population densities in and near cities are very high, most of Japan is actually empty. You can see it as you fly—there is little population or activity outside the cities proper. Japan has large areas of unused mountainous land near cities. In a streetcar-subway-railroad world, which is what the Japanese have had for a long time, you can't use such land. Trains don't run up steep mountain sides. But cars do, and the kind of hilly land which is very desirable in Beverly Hills or Hollywood is as yet unused in Japan. Wait a few years, and if the planners can be persuaded to cooperate by building the roads, sewers, and electric lines, the Japanese will spread out faster than anyone. They have known for centuries how difficult it is to live in extremely high-density situations, and there is hardly a Japanese family that doesn't lust after a bit of grass and a fine garden.

## Conclusion

So we have a real problem and two cities of tomorrow. Why is our first tomorrow not attempted? The answer is simple. In our deepest inner selves, we *want* the 1910 streetcar city. We want to think that everyone wants to live downtown. We believe, counter to all evidence, that all lost functions shortly will return to the city. Although we may never admit it, we might be afraid of a strange world which is imprecise. But we must realize that our present cities were laid out before the automobile, truck, and airplane were well developed. The interrelationships between the new transportation technology and the city, most particularly the private automobile, are very poor. No half-measures or efforts to restore the city to its pre-automobile status are likely to work.

There is one possible alternative. We could eliminate cars, although to do so would require a police state of the sort no one has imagined as yet. We could force trucks off the road, thereby raising transfer costs, lowering our standard of living, and making the poor poorer. We could even return to steam-powered engines and their inherent focus on a highly concentrated industrial core. If we did these things, we could also return to a 1920 standard of living, where over 90 percent of the population was poor by today's definition of poverty. One doubts we like the city that much. We want the best of all possible worlds, but cannot seem to achieve it. Because we cannot chose, we get the worst of each of them —air pollution, inner-city problems, and endless urban crises. Only the future can tell how much we will pay for our mistaken premises about what a city is.

# 5

■ ■

# The Death and Rebirth of the Family Farm

If cities are having some real problems, the family farm doesn't, because it's already dead. In 1884, about half the population lived on farms, and the majority of them were family operations. By 1973, only 5 percent of the population lives on farms, and the number of farmers is still dropping. Only 10 percent of them produce over half the output. There remain only a few marginal farmers of the old breed, and they will soon die off or move to town. The new breed are very good businessmen who happen also to be farmers. The Jeffersonian dream of a sturdy, independent peasantry is over.

The remaining farmers are so successful and good that they can generate surpluses of almost anything, and do, unless some government control prevents it. We often hear worries that the spreading suburbs will take all the farmland, and food supply will fall. Actually, for all practical purposes, there is an endless supply of rural farmland available; our real problem is to stop farmers from creating surpluses, not to get them growing enough to eat. And if we weren't such committed protein eaters, which means we use up feed grains in great quantity and with relative inefficiency to create edible animals, we could be fed by about one half of 1 percent of the population. All developed urban and suburban land in the United States now accounts for about 4 percent of the total; doubling or even tripling the land used this way wouldn't make a particle of difference in producing the food we need.

Where did the family farmers go? To the city, where they helped create that problem, as we shall see. Strangely, the more that left, the higher farm outputs got. What happened?

Since 1884, a lot has happened. It began, in one dimension, with the development of the Department of Agriculture and the various land-grant agricultural schools. These powerful information and research systems, in their efforts to help the family farmer, rather quickly, and at a steadily accelerating pace, not only discovered how to farm better, but, through the farm-county-agent system and innumerable publications, lectures, demonstration farms, and other educational devices, taught good farmers how to be better. That they did so is one key to the demise of the family farm. Who learned what they taught? Not the guy who never listened to the county agent, who never read the carefully prepared USDA pamphlets, who did the job the old way. He missed the bus completely. His neighbor, who did, learned, and kept right on learning. And the smarter he was and the faster he learned, the better he got. And then, when a bad year came, guess who bought up the other, slower farmer and expanded? And guess who gave up and moved to the city, to become an unskilled worker and a city problem?

What was learned? Lots of things about genetics, animal breeding, the biochemistry of plants as applied right out in the field, animal husbandry; input-output relationships and efficiencies; better fertilizer analysis; and a thousand other things that the typical laymen would find incomprehensible. But enough of the techniques worked so that output per man and per acre began to rise, and rose faster than even very productive factories. An increase of 6 percent per year in agricultural productivity is an average for the whole twentieth century, and, given a good year when weather is right and prices are favorable, like 1971, the figure reaches 11 percent! Manufacturing is doing a great job when it gets productivity up maybe 4 percent per man per year.

Another key factor in this productivity race has been the total shift from farm animals to other energy sources. At first, starting slowly around 1910, it was the substitution of oil, in the form of gas, for tractors and trucks and farm cars. This effectively cut the amount of forage needed to feed work animals, to the point where we now need only two-thirds the acreage we used to need—the hay is gone, or used for milk or meat animals. And eager farm-equipment suppliers, finding a good market in improved equipment, continue to improve it to this day, making it bigger, more reliable, and less labor-intensive. Now a South Dakota or Kansas wheat farmer can easily handle 1,000, or even 2,000 acres on his own—instead of the old quarter section of 160 acres. A plot of 160 acres is a quarter of a square mile, and in the 1870s, this was the size of the family farm. By 1947, most farmers had 320. A common sight in South Dakota at that time was every other house abandoned, through the endless square miles of the wheat belt. Now, it is not at all uncommon to find an agribusinessman farming 2,000 acres, using perhaps half a million dollars worth of machinery and equipment. This agribusinessman may still be a family farmer, but he is not exactly what most people have in mind when they talk about the typical family farm.

If you go talk to today's successful farmer, one of the 10 percent who generate half the output, he will be friendly enough, but much of his talk will be incomprehensible, about fertilizer mixes, proper trace elements in the soil, transmission problems with self-propelled combines, and much, much more. He sounds, in short, just like any other skilled businessman-technician doing a very demanding job.

If such men can produce 6 percent more output per year per man and per acre, and if population is increasing only 1 percent per year (or even 1.7 percent per year, as it did in the U.S. as recently as the 1950s), something has got to give. Thus, it is no real surprise to learn that the best years of prosperity for American farmers in the twentieth century have been during and just after world wars, when major food-production areas such as Europe and the Far East were shattered. It was then clear that the American farmer could feed the world, if others wanted to buy his product or if they could figure out how to pay for it. (They still do. American agricultural exports recently have run over eight billion dollars per year). But in more normal times, too much is produced; food prices fall, and farmers are in trouble. The ones in the worst trouble are those who are least productive, so they leave farming and go to the cities. The farmers who remain push for help politically, and historically they have got it.

Political changes are in the wind, since we now have more or less equal and proportional representation in our government, so farmers cannot have quite as much political muscle as they used to. The days when a farm vote was equal to four or five city votes is gone, and with so many fewer farmers and their families around to vote, the political slippage is very noticeable. We really are an urban nation, and slowly we shift laws and pressures to recognize this fact.

But we can't get rid of a half century of laws and ideals about the family farm very quickly, and we still have weird regressive subsidies which reward the rich and punish the poor on the farm. We still have the last trickle of pushed-out farmers, although many fewer than there used to be. And we still have the huge and efficient machinery for learning to be a better farmer, which once again is used extensively by the good farmers, and hardly at all by the poor ones. One of the ironies of farming, among other things, is that when knowledge is subsidized by the state and made available to all, the ones who take full advantage of it tend to be the upper middle classes, who have the education, discipline, profit orientation, and general interest to use it. The poor fellows with less education don't even realize what they miss. Those great agricultural schools in many states are not attended by the sons of poor, marginal farmers, who so badly need the training but by the sons of the very successful farmers, highly subsidized by general tax money, who then go home to do still better. So here we sit, with a bunch of very good agribusinessmen running our few farms, with a bunch of laws structured to help the old-fashioned family farmer, wondering where the dream went. Is it any surprise that, somewhere around 1950, we lost the family farm forever?

But we did not lose the image of the family farm. It survives in at least two ways. One is the agricultural commune. A bunch of young city types, convinced that the world is rotten to the core, move back to the land, hoping to develop a new social form—or perhaps an ancient form in modern guise. All will work together, all will share together. It is an old dream, and there is plenty of farmland out there to try on. So why not? Maybe peace, brotherhood, and prosperity are there, plus even greater and more intangible social and personal gains.

Like so many other radical types in our society, the typical commune volunteer is an ex-upper-middle-class suburban person who has had some college training. Young people who have grown up on farms rarely get involved. They know already what farming is about, and they have had enough—plus the fact that their farm upbringing was not exactly the type best suited for commune living.

So the commune gets started, using traditional ways of cultivation, no machinery, probably no electric power, and all the rest. It's back to 1884, with Lem as the best guide. And very quickly two basic problems crop up. The first is that such farming, if you're serious about making it an economically viable proposition, is incredibly hard work. Someone has to get out there and do the plowing and the rest of the work. The bugs and pests are very real, and no matter what you feel about ecology, to see them eat your own crop can be discouraging. Lem thought so too, but he didn't know what to do about it. And you have to know so much—few of the suburban types have the necessary background in such things as animal husbandry, entomology, and so on to do the job right. The usual result is collapse of the commune.

The second problem is that outputs are so damn low in this kind of farming. Lem made perhaps three hundred dollars per year in a good year in the 1880s, and farm prices, thanks to productivity gains, haven't really gone up much since. Maybe they've doubled. So you make six hundred dollars per year from the same land, and you have a dozen or more people to share the proceeds with in the commune. Winter comes, it gets cold as hell, and the troops drift off. Lem made three hundred dollars only because he specialized in the best crop he could find. If you do general purpose farming, the odds are high that you won't make that much—which is another way of saying that no one can grow enough to feed himself and the horses.

Once in a while a successful farm commune does pop up. In examining it, one can only be struck with admiration for the incredible discipline that exists. Those dedicated people not only work all the time, but they are willing to put up with discomforts that few modern Americans would accept. Incidentally, I've noticed that quite a few successes stem from the fact that one commune member's aunt or grandfather just happened to leave him or her an income of twenty thousand a year, which makes the psuedo-nature of the operation clear. If returning to the land and the family farm means heavy cash subsidies from the rest of us, it hardly seems like the wave of the future.

Other communes have "succeeded" by going commercial. A craft shop is set up by the main road, and commune members sell arts, crafts, and organically grown food at fairly high prices. If this works, then the group is rapidly drawn into the small business net— profits and losses become important, calculations as to what to do become money-oriented—and at this point, the commune becomes just another picturesque business. That hardly seems to be the salvation of man.

The sad fact of the matter is that the old-fashioned family farm, using animal and human power, and based on centuries of collective ignorance about what to do, was a low-income, hard-work, tightly disciplined way of life. You either worked all the time or starved to death. And when a chance came to work in Mr. Ford's auto plant at five dollars a day in 1916, anyone who heard about it jumped at the chance. Sadly enough, it's still the same. Few of us have the guts to live an eighteenth- or nineteenth-century life for real.

The second vestige of the family farm, particularly for the lower-income types, is the part-time farm. Many companies need a good, stable labor supply; many dying farm towns have cheap housing, plus lots of marginal farmers around. So the company builds a plant there, and the farmers come in to work. Because they own cars, the farmer-workers continue to stay on their farms. Why move into town? Besides, on the old family farm, lousy as it is, there are ten or twenty good acres where corn or wheat or something else can be grown. And maybe there is some pastureland where beef cattle can roam. There's real money in beef now, or have you shopped for some recently? So the farmer gets his eight-hour-a-day job as a worker. If the plant closes down for a while, the worker is not too unhappy—he has some fences to mend, a pickup truck to overhaul, and lots of other things to do. It's a good deal all around—the part-time farmer gets extra income, perhaps his wife and children get jobs, and he still lives out on his farm eleven miles from town.

Southern Indiana is full of these part-time farmers. The farmland is poor, but there are spots of bottom land here and there which can produce good incomes, and there is lots of rugged pastureland which is good for a few beef cattle. And when you go to a farm auction in the county, when an old-time farmer is retiring, the premium prices are paid for small 1948 Ford tractors, not the high-powered, totally efficient modern machines. The boys at the auction can't use that big stuff—they are just farming a few acres, down at the home place. I know guys who never finished grade school whose families are in the $20,000-a-year bracket, lots of it tax-free or -exempt. Mama makes $3,500 down at the electronics assembly line; dad makes $5,000 out at another plant; the oldest girl, who lives at home, brings back $4,500 as a clerk-typist at the university; and the family farm generates the rest. No one would call such a family upper middle class —but their income is, and they are happy to earn it. By 1984, many others may have caught on.

As a matter of fact, lots of people are beginning to. One development in the past forty years that helped farmers was the rapid extension of electric lines all over the countryside. Rural Electrification Agencies intended to give the old family farmers the benefits of cheap power, and indeed they did. But they also gave anyone else out there in the country the same benefits. And because rural people now have power, they can have all the electric slaves the city dwellers have. Moreover, such luxuries as air conditioning and all electric heating are possible. So some of us have begun to drift back to the farm, not as professional farmers, but as affluent urbanites who just like to live out there where it's quiet, and where we have lots of room of our own. Instead of wandering around a crowded city park, have your own private park, where you can have your selective privacy. For a few hundred dollars an acre, you can buy a broken-down marginal farm, build a new house, and relax safely in a life style no older farmer would ever have believed. Of course, it helps to have a paved road out to the farm, and once again a program designed to help farmers turns out to help the modern urbanite. In lots of places where it snows, the county will even salt the roads in winter, so you can get in or out even on bad days.

If the roads are a bit poor (which means that the old farm is a lot cheaper), you can buy a jeep or bronco and use the four-wheel drive to get in and out when you have to. Sales of such vehicles have steadily climbed since the war, and not all of them get sold to western ranchers. In some parts of these United States, owning one of the four-wheel drive vehicles is a real status symbol. It may even have replaced the station wagon as an indication that you have arrived.

Farms that city folk buy tend to be very marginal for farming, since such places are always much more scenic than good farms. Good farms, the ones the farm pros want, are flat and dull—poor farms are full of trees, rocks, and gulleys. So the affluent city dweller moves out to the old uneconomic farm and builds a modern house, complete with all the conveniences. If he has some good land, he can rent it to one of the good farmers around and make enough maybe to pay taxes. If he doesn't, he can read the fine print in various tax laws about how to beat the game with timber or soil banks, or something. In any case, he enjoys the rural life, without suffering any of its disadvantages. After all, his income comes from the urban agglomeration, not from the farm. This type of farming life isn't even very expensive in many parts of the United States. In the Midwest, ten thousand dollars will buy you enough acreage (along with some old moldering barns, outhouses, and houses) to feel quite alone in. A new house won't cost much more, and maybe less, than a suburban split-level. Taxes, thanks to the way we have subsidized all those nice old farmers, are likely to be a lot less than in the suburb, and a hell of a lot less than in the city. Of course, you get a lot less in terms of police and fire protection, but you probably won't need it anyhow.

When you have built your dream house out there in the middle of nowhere, often only ten or fifteen miles from town, you can sit back and enjoy the farm life like the older farmers never did. Since you're not farming, there is little work to be done. What work has to be done, like pumping water, heating or cooling the place, doing the clothes, or whatever, is done by those pleasant electric slaves, which get turned off when they are not needed. And if crime rates rise in the city, or there is yet another educational crisis, or the bus drivers go on strike, well that's someone else's problem, not yours. You can leisurely stroll around your ancestral acres, like an English lord, watching the rabbits, seeing where birds nest, enjoying the babbling brook. If you want to restore an antique car, the old barn is ready, and if your saw makes lots of noise, the nearest neighbor will never even hear you. If you have even wilder tastes, such as collecting old steam tractors or full-size railroad cabooses, you can do that too. If you like target shooting, you don't even need a gun permit. And if it gets too hot, go inside where your air conditioning is working and watch color television for a while. In short, live your private, selective life the way you want to live it. Since no one else is around, you don't have to worry whether the neighbors or the police mind. As long as you don't scare the horses, you can do just about anything you damn well please. And that *is* freedom.

So far, this trend is for the affluent, the upper 10 or 20 percent. But wait until 1984—by then, the roads will be better, the electric lines will go to still more improbable places; the cesspool engineers will have come up with still better ways of getting rid of the sewage; and lots of us will have higher incomes. We may also have much more leisure. And if we want to go farming in the modern manner, then why not? The model is there—it's the English fifteenth-century manor house we see from time to time on the late show, and who doesn't want to live like a lord?

The real family farm is dead, and nothing can bring it back. But a surprisingly large number of us city slickers seem to like the babbling brook, the rocks, the trees, and all the rest, so, given income, options, transportation, and communications, we may just go back to the farm. Those who actually grew up on farms, and who know how much work it involved, will smile, but we won't be bothered. It's our farm and our fun, and we can leave it at that.

# 6

■ ■

# *Vocational Choice*

"What's your training?"

"Nothing," I told her, "that does me any good. I had an education that was supposed to fit me for the appreciation of art, literature, and life. It didn't have anything to do with making money. I find that I can't appreciate art, literature, or life without money."*

You're at a pleasant party, and, as usual, you chat with lots of new people. A nice young man talks to you for a while, introduces himself, and finally asks, "What do you consume?"

Most Americans would find this a weird question. The expected one is, "What do you do?" And the odd note the consumption question strikes suggests that for most

*Erle Stanley Gardner, *The Bigger They Come* (New York: Pocket Books, 1963) p. 3.

of us, our vocation is perhaps the most important factor in our lives. We all need roles, and the more prestigious and well-paying the role, the better we like it. There is a world of difference between, "I'm a doctor," and, "Oh, right now I'm unemployed." Indeed, most people, when asked their vocation, will lie a bit. Garbage men become sanitation engineers; teachers become research professors; general practitioners become medical specialists.

In spite of many discussions about how it really isn't going to be necessary to do as much work as before, we are still going to be working in 1984. The freedom instruments are relatively expensive, and few of us are lucky enough to have an independent income. Well over 99 percent of all families have to work to get the good life, if they want it. Those who don't work, either involuntarily, as when a person is unemployed, or voluntarily, as when a student drops out, are always suspect. Americans don't like bums, and they are suspicious of those who somehow can't find work, even though from 4 to 6 percent of the work force will be involuntarily unemployed at any given time. Both self-esteem and the good life require a career, however humble.

The increasing number of women who work are part of the trend. Historically, a woman's place was in the home, but now over 40 percent of women have careers, and by 1984 this percentage will probably have risen. It is still respectable for a woman to stay home and keep house, but it is equally respectable for her to go out and work. Lack of job opportunities of the right type, rather than social attitudes, seem presently to be the limiting factor. Given the consumption options available, it makes sense for many families to put the wife to work— or to have her eagerly volunteer for it. After all, electric slaves cut short her housework routines.

Note that our culture has some peculiar views of what work and careers are. If you keep house, you're not working, although anyone who has done it knows how tough this can be. If you fix your own electric wiring, you're not working, even if you can do things that skilled electricians do. No, work is structured, usually involving working for someone else for money. We ignore 4 million farmers and the 4.5 million small businessmen (including millions of self-employed professionals, such as medical doctors, lawyers, consulting engineers, and economists).

What has been happening all through the twentieth century is a steady expansion of work roles. In 1884 and before, we all knew who did what, since there were few roles to perform, and we could watch most of them. We knew what farmers, lawyers, doctors, carpenters, and laborers did. But as the world grew more complex and specialized, the number of job classifications exploded. Many jobs are now very mysterious to the outsider. What does a cyberneticist do? Something useful and well paid, to be sure, but few young people, pondering a career, know, nor can they perceive the entry route to this profession. The only obvious thing about such a job is that it requires a very high level of education. Indeed, most of today's jobs require skill and training levels far above anything known historically, and traditional professional jobs, such as those in medicine, also involve much more education than before.

So, if you want to get a good job in a demanding field, which pays well enough to obtain the nice consumer things, the way to do this is to get educated. Many studies have suggested that there is a pretty good relationship between education, income, and status. Young people in any generation, being very perceptive about such things, go on to college to advance. And up to now, this has been a pretty good strategy. In fact, it has been so good that we now find over 45 percent of eighteen-year-olds going on to some form of higher education, a trend made possible by massive investments in the state colleges and universities. As recently as 1946, only about 12 percent of the eighteen-year-olds went on after high school.

More recent studies have suggested that perhaps this relationship between education and income is not all that absolute. Clearly there are class barriers which prevent bright but poor young people from reaching the top, and if your family was working-class, just going on from some dreary high school to the cow college does not guarantee success. If your parents know people and are upper middle class, your chances after getting a good education improve dramatically.

But as usual, what else is there? The bright poor young man or woman, contemplating a career, has no chance at all, except possibly in starting their own small businesses, without a good education. Even small businessmen these days often have advanced training in business subjects. So, off to college, with hopes. Perhaps you won't end up as vice-president of the big company, or senior civil servant in the government bureaucracy, but at least you won't end up sweeping the floor, or working on the assembly line.

Nevertheless, enough bright young people are questioning the traditional premise that education equals success so that the rate of increase of college enrollments is slowing down. Significantly, the more vocationally oriented schools, where education leads directly to jobs, are growing. Within the universities, the professional schools, where jobs wait at the end of training, are growing, while more liberal-arts-oriented programs, where nothing much is visible at the end of the line, are declining.

These facts suggest that the game may start changing quite significantly in the 1970s. Historically, around 50 to 60 percent of the college starters finished a four-year

program, so twenty-five years ago, perhaps 6 percent of
the twenty-two-year-olds were college graduates. These
fortunate young people did get the cream of the jobs.
Where specific professional training was involved, as in
medicine, accounting, or law, the college-trained people
of 1950 were taking virtually all the good jobs. And studies of key high-level executives and administrators
through the years have suggested that the majority of the
new arrivals at the top have college educations, and often
graduate training as well. But as more and more young
people start college and finish it, a new problem arises.
If 50 percent start, this means, given present dropout
rates, that about 25 percent of our twenty-two-year-olds
will have college degrees. And it is hard to figure out, in
any meaningful way, how 25 percent of any group can be
an elite.

So we have a new pattern. Young people trained in
specific professional things, such as medicine and optometry, still get jobs, but liberal-arts-trained generalists
have trouble. And they are likely to stay in trouble. What
has happened is that the traditional university or college
is largely process-oriented, reflecting its slowly evolving
philosophy through many centuries. Historically, university education was for an elite, and a very small one at
that. To learn to savor and enjoy all of Western culture
was something that only well-placed people, economically and socially, were able to do. If, upon graduation,
they wanted to work, they were the ones who could
handle the intellectual abstractions, the information
searches, and the model-building necessary in the complex organizations of their day. Hence many of the senior managers and administrators of large organizations
had liberal-arts backgrounds in good schools. Incidentally, having an uncle or cousin or father who could
arrange the proper introductions to the persons doing
the hiring helped, too.

Although the liberal-arts game was already coming to an end in the 1950s, new problems were obscured both by voracious demands for teachers at all levels, which conveniently employed many liberal-arts graduates, and by the explosion of white-collar and highly technical work in all its aspects. Many organizations are now structured more like eggs than pyramids—in the bulging middle are the white-collar types, the design engineers, librarians, economists, financial planners, personnel specialists, computer programmers, inventory planners, and all the rest of the new types who fit the organizational hierarchy. And many of these types, if not the majority, have been to college.

Two things have begun to happen which will make this particular game very different from now on into the 1980s. One is the collapse of the teaching market—already we have huge surpluses of teachers, thanks to lower birthrates and budget crunches in many school districts; the other is that many organizations have discovered how to get along with fewer middle-level people used more efficiently. And while the market for liberal-arts graduates expands steadily, it does not appear to be expanding enough, so the historic patterns of college-student placement will be changed by 1984.

What it adds up to is deep trouble for the traditional class-jumping educational exercise so many older Americans know all about. You go to high school and do better than your father, who only finished grade school. Then your kids go to college, and they do better than you do—but for some large number of young people between now and 1984, it won't work anymore.

Young people are not unperceptive on this point, nor are older ones who sense that they are in dead-end jobs. So what are they doing? They are turning to an output-oriented sort of education. What the vast majority want out of their school or college is a good job at good pay, not a careful study of the Western world or insights into the philosophy of man. So the institutions to watch, and the ones already growing as fast as they can expand, are the trade schools, commercial colleges, and junior colleges with vocational programs. In 1971, for the first time in many years, freshman enrollment actually declined in four-year colleges, and it declined again in 1972. If the colleges can't provide for the good economic life, then the students are looking for some school that will. And they are likely to continue to do so for the rest of the decade.

This trend has been going on quietly for a century. Every city has its commercial college, a profit-making organization, where young people are taught typing, shorthand, and other marketable skills. And every issue of *Popular Mechanics* and *Mechanix Illustrated* for decades has carried ads for quite reputable and good correspondence schools such as International Correspondence Schools and the Alexander Hamilton Institute. Examination of their ads over the years reveals one interesting characteristic—these schools will teach you anything that pays off in the market. And if a new field comes along, like electronics or computer programming, numerous other schools, all profit-making, are quickly in the game. Of course, all of this is not quite intellectually respectable, but these schools operate under one constraint that more traditional schools do not have—if they can't satisfy their students, they go broke, and fast. And the fact that they are expanding very rapidly, while other kinds of schools are not doing too well, suggests that a lot of people out there want education for use, not for fun and games.

One major reason for all the interest in more highly skilled jobs is that the less skilled ones are declining in numbers. The old-fashioned, mind-numbing, monotonous assembly-line type of work is gradually disappearing, either to automation or overseas, where somebody is willing to do it for less money. Busboys, elevator operators, and other low-level employees are automated out of work, a major reason why teen-age and poverty-group unemployment rates are so high. These are the workers who haven't got the skills to get and hold more productive jobs. There has been a steady trend to more brains and less brawn in work for a long time now, and there is no evidence to suggest that this trend won't continue. Already, well over half the labor force doesn't work physically—it thinks. And thinking, of the right sort, pays a lot more than doing.

Training in thinking, when added to such items as cars and telephones, also gives a person another kind of freedom, which is the ability to move to the job, wherever it is. Most skilled workers are soon into a job network of some sort, which might be area-wide (as in various crafts), or even nationwide (as in some professions such as college teaching). If your present job peters out or appears to offer no real future, then get into the information net and find out what else is available. Perhaps halfway across the country, someone needs a person of exactly your talents. So, you apply, fly or drive to a job interview, take the position, pack up, and move to the job. Highly skilled professionals have the income, cars, and information to do this, while unskilled persons find it very difficult. They tend to stay where they are. About a third of all Americans move every year. It figures— what is happening is that if a person has highly skilled and sellable talent, he or she normally has the ability to sell it just about anyplace. And once again, we find new freedom and new options open to many people. This mobility seems certain to increase by 1984. Travel and communication are certain to be cheaper. When people have options, they use them. And since higher incomes and more interesting jobs are clearly things people want, we can expect lots of girls and fellows to take advantage of new options.

Such mobility may well be another nail in the coffin of the real world of 1940. Rapidly increasing mass mobility tears apart the traditional structured society. Indeed, moving from a village or town where everyone knows everyone else, and where lots of your life is public, to an apartment or house which is largely private, has the effect of blocking off many persons from public-oriented life. They pick up the freedom instruments and immediately use them wherever they are, in whatever way they want, without fear of the displeasure of suspicious neighbors, peers, and superiors. Which is one of the major reasons, come to think about it, why so many people are quite willing to pull up stakes and go someplace else. It may be fun for the upper classes to have a bunch of subservient peons around forever, but the peons, interested in advancing themselves, feel that the best thing to do is bail out—and they do.

Like so many other things we have discussed, mobility is really not very new. The whole history of the United States is a study in people milling around. The key difference is in numbers. When virtually everyone can or does move wherever he or she wants to get a job and live, we suddenly discover that the world is very different from when only a small percentage moved around. Our cherished notions of stability, order, and knowing what's going on and who's who tend to collapse, and many of us feel very lonesome in a world of strangers. Then learned scholars write books pointing out how dismal the lives of these mobile people are, without roots, without family, without concept of their history. No one ever asks if the people moving around are enjoying themselves. Yet even casual discussions with those supposedly unhappy people suggest that they are having a ball.

By 1984, lots of people who now are stuck in one job

in one area may be able to join those who already have
mobility. Craftsmen, factory workers, and other less
professionally oriented people have sometimes moved,
but only at some risk since they had first to go somewhere and then find a job. By 1984, the scenario might
be something like this:

A young lady from a frigid northern city takes one
more look at all that snow and ice in January and decides
that she's had it. She goes to an employment-placement
service (which may be public, but more likely than not is
private) and applies for job information. She's now working at a clerical job, and she has various skills, which are
recorded. The agency performs a master search across
the whole country (or only the South or California or
Florida or wherever the young lady specifies) and within
a few seconds all available jobs which match the lady's
qualifications are printed out on computer tape. She
finds that business is lousy in California, and there are no
good jobs, but that Atlanta offers a few which seem quite
interesting.

She then applies for an interview by television telephone, talks to the boss, and they both consider if it's a
good match. The boss likes what he sees, and offers her
the job, but before she takes it, she asks the agency for
further information. Within a microsecond or two, she
gets her second computer printout, which includes all
sorts of the usual Chamber of Commerce information—
apartment costs, road maps, food prices, advice on what
clothes to wear, and so on. After some study, she decides
to take the job. She resigns that afternoon, hops in her
car, and drives six hundred miles down the interstate
freeway for ten or twelve hours to her new destination.
Of course, the computer in the agency has also given her
a list of apartment rentals, restaurants, and other information which can help her settle in rapidly at minimum
inconvenience. When she arrives, Atlanta's reception

committee, which has been informed of her arrival, meets her, helps her arrange banking facilities, housing, and all the rest, and tries to make their new (taxpaying) citizen feel at home.

Meanwhile, a young lady in Florida, who loves skiing and other winter sports, is thinking about moving up north. She goes to the agency in her city and gets the news that a job up north is available . . .

Instead of quitting, going blindly to some other city or town, then spending much time looking for a job, maybe without success, people using this system would find it not only economically efficient, but also nice to use. If the whole process cost a hundred dollars or perhaps less, lots of people would use it. Someone could make some money without trying too hard.

For a few high-paid, very high-skill professionals, most of this placement net is already in operation, so it is not too hard to forecast that it will continue to expand to other types of jobs. Except for the TV telephone interview, everything else is now around—it is a problem of getting organized, not of inventing new technology or ideas.

If you yearn for the old small-town life, where no one ever went anyplace, and where everyone knew everyone else, you're in the wrong world. The reason is simple— if you're stuck, you move if you can. An almost forgotten characteristic of the old, stable, less mobile small town is that most people *were* stuck. Thanks to modern communication and transportation, they are not stuck any more. The trend to more and more people having more and more options will continue, and already manpower planners are seeing the need to build nationwide (or even worldwide) information and forecasting systems to utilize all manpower more effectively. By 1984 we should have some sort of national manpower forecast, along with a national job-information system. Workers' options will be a lot better than they now are, and they will have more freedom.

The steady trend to education for use will also have some other interesting effects. Already, one upstate Michigan high school has tried the intriguing experiment of going around the Midwest, interviewing employers to find out exactly what they wanted, and then training their students to fill exactly those jobs. The response was typical and expected—citizens felt it was disgraceful for the school to push students out from their home town (which had a 30-percent-plus teen-age unemployment rate), and educators found the idea of educating a person only for his work distasteful. The plan worked, though, for lots of students, and we will see a lot more of this because a real problem through 1979 is the steadily increasing number of young people coming on the labor market each year. Moreover, we will likely have real problems in placing displaced workers and less skilled workers, too. If we can figure out what we need in the way of manpower, and we can train workers quickly and cheaply to meet these needs, then we will all be better off, most specifically including the people who find better jobs.

Closely related to educating for employment is the fact that many fewer persons feel the need to learn what the universities have traditionally taught. There was a time, and not too long ago, when there was only a limited range of acceptable leisure pursuits—the theater, opera, reading, music, and so on. A truly educated man was expected to know about, participate in, and enjoy these things. But the avocational explosion has meant, among other things, that quite sophisticated and well-educated people can enjoy things which in the past would have been regarded as weird, unsound, crude, and even unethical. So who ever heard of a college offering courses in motorcycle hopping-up, foundry practice, camping, or antique-car rebuilding? There are perhaps some distantly related disciplines, but nothing right on target. The person who enjoys these activities neither worries much about nor feels the lack of his appreciation and knowledge of great literature or music. He's simply marching to a different drummer.

Much of this sort of cultural involvement is not even considered by intellectuals. To them it is neither good nor bad—just totally irrelevant. But anyone who has bothered to spend some time with people who are doing something not quite nice in the educated-man sense quickly realizes that to the participants such things are very relevant indeed. If the intellectual establishment doesn't pay any attention, then the participants won't reciprocate either.

Another related point is that colleges don't change much—they still use the same lecture system practiced in the Middle Ages. But the students can and do get information all over the place—mainly on TV, but there are also huge quantities of books, magazines, newspapers, and other written stuff being sold, and maybe even being read. One dimension of the new freedom is the ability to get at all sorts of information in many forms. If someone wants to find out about model railroading or antique autos, he can now afford (if he has a job) to buy specialist journals. If colleges think his interests are irrelevant, then why go? Better to go to the trade school or junior college, get a good technical job, and do one's avocational thing, whatever it may be.

It is worth noting that there is beginning to be a curious split between vocations and avocations. Some people work all the time. Many professionals (medical doctors, lawyers), administrators, managers, and high-level technical people live this way. Carrying home the well-filled briefcase is a part of the American folklore. So do writers, for whom the task is never done, along with

other media people, such as TV writers and newspaper-
men. Eighty- or ninety-hour work weeks are a part of the
game, and if one cuts such a person off from work, he
tends to get nervous quite quickly. The typical characteristic of this sort of work is its lack of closure—no matter
what you do, there is always more to do than one can
handle.

Another group of workers are essentially time-clock
punchers, although few of these really punch the clock.
They put in their eight hours, walk off the job, and forget
it until the next day. And this group leaves vocational
cares and responsibilities behind when they go home.
They have the time and interest to do avocational things.
Since we are not all going to be chiefs at work, lots of
people decide very early in the game to do something
which is reasonably enjoyable and interesting too. Such
people drift off into the literally thousands of avocations
which generally pass unnoticed by everyone except the
aficionados. But they are very easy to find, if you look.
The trouble is that few look, and one result is a very
distorted image of what America really is these days.

The very nature of American work is changing very
fast. Serious industrial relations and personnel experts
these days are suggesting that it may well be impossible
to continue doing the old-fashioned, monotonous, pro-
duction-line kinds of work in the United States much
longer—there just aren't enough unskilled, un-
dereducated, high-boredom-tolerance people around
any more. General Motors' experience with its Lords-
town, Ohio, plant is perhaps very significant. A major
new facility was built in the traditional style, and the
company apparently cannot find enough of the old types
of workers to make the place run reasonably well. The
numbers of labor disputes, wildcat strikes, and whatnot
over the past few years has led many industrialists to
wonder if such a thing can be done anywhere in the
United States.

One result of such experiences is that we should see steady progress in the field of job enlargement, actually nothing more than having workers expand the work task to make it more interesting and relevant. Instead of soldering one connection forever, the electronics worker assembles the whole system. Instead of tightening fourteen bolts on one engine all day, the worker might assemble a whole series of components and get them properly installed. Instead of answering one type of complaint letter, the worker might answer dozens of different queries. All of these job enlargements have the effect of making workers think more, be more creative, and use whatever skills they have, and they tie nicely into the kinds of workers we now have in the United States. Such concepts have been around for decades, but to date in most cases firms have felt that such efforts cost more in supervision and planning than they gained. Until now, there were lots of low-skill people around to do the job in the old way. But by 1984, there may not be.

Another related development is the changing structure of work hours. We all got used to the forty-hour, five-day week about forty years ago, during the Great Depression. Before that, we were all used to the forty-eight or even up to sixty-hour, six-day week. By now, virtually all workers have been at a forty-hour week for all their working lives. That's the way it is. But a few years back, various employers began experimenting with odd hours and times. How about a forty-hour week, of four ten-hour days? Of maybe a forty-hour week where you come in on Mondays and Wednesdays, but work at home the rest of the time? Or maybe a forty-hour week, but you only work every other week, or maybe half the year, or something? Various experiments with oddball hours have suggested that workers really want flexibility. Firms that have seriously tried such experiments have discovered that they can cream the labor market by offering such deals. The attraction of every weekend being a three-day holiday intrigues many who don't mind working ten hours a day for the other four. Lawyers, writers, professors, and other professionals have long worked when they wanted to. I have professorial friends who do most of their "work" between three and six in the morning; some who work best in a corner of the local bar; some who religiously come in every day at eight and leave at five; and some who work at night with the TV on and the sound turned off. It really doesn't matter. Their sort of creative, unstructured work can be accomplished almost anyplace, anytime.

The lucky people who name their own hours tend to have one thing in common—whatever they are doing, it is almost impossible to structure their work according to some rigid work-rule formula. How long does it take a Perry Mason to figure out a perfect defense in a murder case? How long does it take a lawyer to get an inspired thought about how to defend a client from an antitrust suit? A day? A month? Five years? As long as this man does his job, it doesn't really matter. How, when, or where he does it is irrelevant. Increasingly, with the trend to *thinking* jobs rather than *doing* jobs, it should be possible to think at odd hours and odd locations.

This inevitable trend makes highly structured bosses nervous, but increasingly we are recognizing that much of what we call work ill fits the standard concepts of work day and place. Indeed, if you lock the lawyer up in his office, he may well be less productive. Lots of people do their best thinking out on the golf course, or fiddling around in their garden. The trend is clear. Increasingly we have more think work, plus more need for creative people to do it. Lots of work is going to be done some way other than the historic way. We also are getting increasingly sophisticated about how to measure work. We used to see a man making a part for some machine, and we knew exactly what he did. We could also count the parts he made, and we knew that he needed the plant machinery to do his job. Now we are beginning to measure much more subtle kinds of work against performance norms, and this means that people who now sit around offices for eight hours a day may well be able to sit around home.

## 1984 Scenario

A woman who has small children both wants to do complex work and needs the salary. Before her marriage, she had worked for a number of years in an office, and she is well aware of most office routines. So she gets a job (using the national job-information service). Every day, her company mails her a sheaf of customer complaint letters. She sorts them out, answers the easy ones on her own electric typewriter (it's hard to remember that even twenty years ago, a home typewriter was a rarity, and electrics were unknown). Then she takes a close look at the more complicated ones. She calls various company personnel (some of whom may also be at home, or in their summer cottages, or whatever) on her TV telephone and asks them questions to get the necessary facts. Then she polishes off her answers. Using her company-owned stamp machine, she addresses them, sticks them in envelopes, and drops them off in the corner mailbox. Better yet, she may well just send the letters to the company's clients via closed circuit teletype direct to their home or place of business.

Every so often, this lady gets called away from her work by other things, like sick children. Then she does her work at night or on Sundays. It really doesn't matter to the company that pays her as long as the work gets done within a few days of receipt of the complaint. It takes her four hours to finish the job on an average day, but she gets paid for eight. The company, before hiring her, did a careful work study of this job and set a reasonable norm. Then, just to be on the safe side, it added 50 percent to what had been accomplished in the usual eight-hour day, and let this lady know that if she handled that much work, she had done her eight-hour day. Since this lady has lots of other things she wants to do and can do, she works fast and well. The company audits her work from time to time, and it also picks up feedback from salesmen about whether or not dissatisfied customers are now satisfied. As it turns out, she's doing much better than the people she replaced down at the office. And back at the office, people are pleased too. The company saves the rent on a few hundred square feet of office space, which at today's rates is worth saving, and they get a sticky job done well by a woman who ordinarily would not even be in the labor market. Both time and money are saved. By 1984, we should be seeing lots more of this kind of work.

We are just going to have to get used to new ideas about what work is. Women have sat at home and written letters for a long time, but not for money. This wasn't work, no matter how sophisticated the letters were. Writing letters for a company at home is work. But since this lady can have visitors, take an hour off to shop, pick up the kids at school, or do almost anything she wants, somehow it doesn't seem like work. Increasingly, we are beginning to recognize that for many kinds of work, the classical structure simply isn't necessary. What is necessary is some means of figuring out how to measure output at a distance, so that the oddball worker can get paid properly for work done. And we can and will get used to men wandering around during "working" hours, women sitting on beaches doing something for money, and all the rest.

Institutional difficulties are more likely to slow up this

trend more than anything. Most of our laws regulating work were passed many years ago, when work was highly structured and everyone was in the factory where he belonged. Right now, most pension funds are not trans- ferrable, so if a person changes jobs in his early forties or fifties, he can lose a lot of future pension money. And most part-time workers do not have the fringe benefits that full-time workers do. But change is coming—already many teachers and professors have a pension system which can be transferred between employers, and other groups are pressing for similar advantages. Unions and legislators are beginning to work toward giving various part-time workers the same fringe benefits that other workers get. By 1984 we should see a much more fluid labor market, where a person who moves may not have to give up so much of his future to do so, and where part-time workers have the same rights as full-time work- ers. Pressure to equalize women's rights help here, since so many part-time workers are female.

Work is rapidly being restructured in another way. More and more, jobs require some creativity. Perhaps half the American work force has some creative compo- nent built into its jobs, and 10 percent are extremely creative. In 1884, perhaps 2 percent were creative. By 1984, lots more work will be creative, simply because creative work can be so much more productive than the traditional kind. Now, one order you just can't give to anyone is, "Be creative!" You as a boss can say it, but your words are meaningless. You can see this very clearly in medicine—hospital administrators (who might, in other organizations, be the boss) don't tell doctors what to do, the doctors tell the administrator what to do. Creative writers don't get told what to write—they write what they want. This is one major reason why job en- largement is viewed with suspicion in many quarters, incidentally—if the workers are responsible for their jobs, and they have to be creative about them, what can you do to get them working? What you have to do is to structure the environment so that people feel like being creative. Doing that is a lot harder than just putting the squeeze on by threatening to fire people, or cut pay, or impose some other form of traditional discipline more suitable to the classical dark satanic mill.

So where does this leave us in 1984? In discussing all the problems involving work in the United States, we often overlook the fact that 94 percent or so of the work force is employed; that perhaps 75 to 85 percent of it at any given time is reasonably well satisfied; and that productivity and pay per person steadily rises. We tend to forget the steadily increasing tendency of women to be involved in formal work, which adds up to a double-barreled boost to money incomes. Not only will more productive workers be better paid, but more wives will also be paid too. And there is no real question that Americans will manage to figure out how to spend the extra money—they now feel somewhat deprived at a median family-income of $10,200 per year, and when that median gets up to $16,000 (in 1973 dollars), or more, as it probably will in 1984, most people will still feel deprived.

Since the 1930s, we have been reading about how we no longer have to worry about work, since there is not enough of it to go around. Moreover, we are so rich that it really is silly to worry about doing more work. And more recently, we are told that work tends to pollute, so if we work more, we pollute more. Hence we should start (like yesterday) preparing for more leisure. We should restructure society to consume, perhaps, but certainly not to work.

Yet in spite of all these warnings, admonitions, and caveats, most of us still rather like working. Work gives us a role, a feeling of importance in the general scheme of things. It disciplines us in a way we rather enjoy being disciplined. And very importantly, it gives us the income to do whatever we want when we are not working. When done in moderation, it is also a freedom instrument. This follows from the creative nature of much work—if one thing we really want to do is accomplish something in life, a good creative and meaningful job gives us this opportunity.

I once talked to a skilled engineer who had done very creative work in low-temperature physics. One of his inventions was a long tube which could be deep-frozen at the tip. It was picked up quickly by surgeons, who used the device to freeze off certain brain cells which were causing Parkinson's disease. Within a few years, thousands of sufferers from this trembling disease had been cured. To watch this engineer as he showed pictures and slides of such operations suggested why work really was such a freedom instrument. He had been personally responsible for the well-being of thousands of previously incurable persons. The lucky worker who does something that matters, perhaps only a small thing for any man or woman, as when the machinist makes that key part for some mechanical heart; when the lawyer finally draws the contract that makes something really important happen; when the businessman finally gets on the market the gadget that makes babies happier; or when the optometrist grinds a special lens at long last so the nearly blind man can see—such things are very much a part of our freedom.

Too many people still work at dreary, dull jobs without meaning, but their numbers are falling steadily. We badly need to develop more creative jobs, more jobs with real meaning for both society and the individual. Such jobs mean as much to any human as all the leisure and avocations in the world ever will. They give us interesting companions, the ability to do our thing while working constructively, and the chance to see more of the world through our working experience.

"What do you do?" We've been asking the question for a century or more, and we'll ask it in 1984. The answers may be still more incomprehensible as the kinds of work explode in their complexity, but the question will still be highly relevant. Indeed, the ability to answer it meaningfully is still going to be perceived as one of the more important freedom instruments of all.

# 7

## ■ ■

# *Avocations: Doing Your Thing*

Over sixty years ago, Thorstein Veblen wrote *The Theory of the Leisure Class*. His theme was simple enough: affluent, upper-class people had to invent leisure-time activities to use up the time they were unable or unwilling to use working. The more opulent your leisure-time activities, the more impressive you were. Of course, at the time he wrote, when factory hands and clerks worked sixty hours a week and farmers worked more than that, only a minute fraction of the population expected to have leisure in abundance, so in effect anyone who had leisure was either a bum or very upper-class and stinking rich. Either way, leisure was suspect. The book struck a chord in up tight, hard-working, Calvinist America. Indeed, many foreign critics still note the inability of many Americans to enjoy leisure even now. We run around frantically searching for something to do all the time. Leisure just doesn't seem to fit the American pattern.

But we increasingly have lots of it. Mass leisure really came out of the Great Depression in the 1930s, when not only did many workers have plenty of involuntary unemployment, but many, if not most others, found themselves working a forty-hour week, or less. What were they supposed to do with all those extra hours? No one ever gave them orders, although plenty of writers gave much, much advice. But most Americans, as usual, given the size of their purses, their own inclinations, and the opportunities available, began to use up their leisure in their own ways. Since 1950, the environment has become increasingly fertile for extra avocational activities. Each year, more people have more money above and beyond subsistence needs, and each year, thanks to the slowly increasing numbers of holidays and paid vacations, more time is available. We now even have workaholics, people who just work all the time. Such people usually are engaged in open-ended jobs, such as writing, planning, or other creative work. Whatever is done is inadequate and incomplete—there is always plenty more to do. Moreover, such work is interesting and fun, so the workaholic keeps right on working and wonders once in a while how those other guys and girls seem to have so much time.

Another group of nonleisure types are those who think they need the money. In some cases where a person has a job which gives him lots of time off, we find him moonlighting. Hence in some rubber industry towns, where a thirty-six-hour work week has been common for a long time, a surprisingly large percentage of the workers have another job. They work in service stations on weekends, do guard duty, sell peanuts at ball games, guard supermarkets, and do just about anything else you could think of which can be done off normal working hours. Indeed, this phenomenon is so widespread that one sure prediction if we do get to thirty- or even twenty-hour work weeks is that perhaps a third or more of the work force will find another job to go with their regular one. Such people may also work because they can't think of anything better to do, or because they enjoy work. But work they will, often for eighty or more hours per week.

In a work-oriented economy, no one really looks in depth at avocations. One thing that has happened is that possibilities for various types of leisure-time use have simply exploded. Historically, you could read, go to a play, just sit, maybe hunt if you were out on the farm, or walk around. Travel was expensive and reserved largely for Veblen's upper crust. But in modern America, you can do almost anything, and a whole new set of subcultures are pretty major industries in their own right. Because the United States has never paid much attention to controlling light industries, the market works very well in this area—if someone wants something, and it pays to make it, it gets made. Tom Wolfe has spotted this subcultural development very well. He talks about the motorcycle crew, the pumphouse gang, and all the rest of the weird and wonderful ways of spending time. Indeed, in many cases, leisure and work blend so closely as to become indistinguishable. A young man buys a motorcycle for fun, gets involved in the subculture, and ends up working (playing?) sixteen hours a day in some specialty shop where the cycles are rebuilt.

One characteristic of modern American leisure is exactly this blending of work and play. Historically, work was so physically hard for most people, and hours were so long, that one just sat still after finishing each day's work. But think-work does not take so much out of a person since it involves little or no physical effort. So today's worker has the energy and time to do physical things, craft things, or whatever. Moreover, many an American enjoys doing something creative, such as making a bookcase, taking a hike for a specified distance, making camp at a given spot, or filling out his collection.

This sort of "work" has closure, which our real work often does not.

Closure is the ability to see what one has done in complete form. If you make that bookcase, you finish it, sooner or later. You can see what you have done, put it in your house, and admire it from time to time. The job has been *completed.* A hunter gets his quarry (or doesn't, which is another kind of mission completion); the craftsman finishes his article; the choir finishes its song; the boy-scout leader sees his young men move on to adulthood and win awards; and the motorcycle rebuilder gets his engine going. Most of the time, one knows what he has done. Formal work often lacks such closure: one works in some office, processing documents he will never see again, for purposes which no one bothered to explain. A worker fixes up or makes some minor part in some subassembly which goes into a finished product he will never see. Much professional work also lacks closure —the teacher thinks that he may have done something for his pupils, but he or she can never be sure. Since many people like to finish things and cannot do this at work, they pick an avocation which has a known payoff, which can be completed. And such play gradually becomes as important, if not more important, than the work one does for a living. Lots of Americans just put in workdays so they can get back home and do what's important. Often such play (work?) starts out part-time, and then becomes a full-time activity. The inveterate antique collector opens a shop; the car tinkerer ends up as a mechanic; the model builder gets his own hobby shop; and the gun fan opens a small repair service.

The enormous growth in avocational activities suggests that most people really need work even if they consider it play. The experience of the idle, titled English lord, who doesn't have to hold down a job, and who rather rapidly decays into alcoholism, or maybe worse, is

repeated again and again by persons fortunate enough
not to need a salary. And because a lot of the jobs we do
these days are very specialized, we often need something
more fulfilling to do. As hours of work have gradually
shortened and vacations lengthened, more people find
that they can do something else—and they do. We will
see more of this blending of work and play by 1984.

## *A 1984 Scenario*

A young man discovers that really interesting jobs are
rather hard to find. But he can get a job as an assembler
for some electronics company at a pretty good rate of
pay and he knows he doesn't have to do it forever. Since
wages have been rising around 5 percent per year (after
correction for inflation), he finds that he can make $4.80
per hour in this routine job. What he really finds fulfilling
is tinkering with snowmobiles, since he lives up in Michigan. So he sets up a shop in his garage, contacts all sorts
of people who are equally interested, and goes to "play."
His play consists of lots of studying about engines, re-
working carburetors to get better performance, messing
around with ignition systems, and so on. After a few
years of "playing," the young man has a pretty good set
of tools, including some power equipment he picked up
secondhand from an old auto garage. By now, he can
rebuild anyone's snowmobile, and make it perform better than new. Gradually, he begins to attract customers.
Since all of this is fun, he charges very low prices, and of
course he isn't about to cheat any friend by sticking in
unnecessary parts. Since it's 1984, the electronics job is
no more than a six-hour day, and, moreover, our young
friend has his choice of flexible schedules. So he decides
to work his thirty-hour week in three ten-hour days, and
spends the other four playing with snowmobiles. Before

long, he's making more money playing than working. His total work-play week is around seventy hours, but who cares? He's having a ball. Moreover, his income is way above what any typical factory worker can get. When he gets married, he'll want more time, so he chucks his job at the electronics plant and spends all his time "playing."

Because so many people obviously enjoy this sort of life, we can expect to see more of them living it. Sluggish growth in really creative, high-paying jobs will also push us farther along this path, since many persons will find their creativity better expressed in their avocations. But since the avocation often becomes the vocation, we are not really sure what work means anymore. One delightful thing about avocations is that though you may be stuck in an income-producing job, you can do anything you want avocationally. Maybe the world does not cry for another serious painter, but if you have a passion for painting landscapes, along with the time and income to buy the paint, go ahead. You may someday get good enough to have your own show, but even if you don't, you have still had lots of fun.

These various leisure subcultures have some interesting points in common. Many of them interfere with others not at all, or at least minimally. The fellows who paint because they like it use up infinitesimal amounts of natural resources. Whether their paintings are good or bad is largely irrelevant to the rest of us. Stamp collectors can become really expert amateurs, but their precious collections are of no great interest to nor do they interfere with noncollectors. He who plays chamber music with a few friends might possibly disturb a neighbor now and then, but such interference is minimal. The man who makes pottery or cabinets in his basement also might bother a neighbor, but not often. Note, incidentally, how a noise-making activity fits into the suburban pattern so well. And that's where the subcultures normally are. It is a lot less bothersome to run a band saw in the basement of your separate house than it is to do it in your high-rise apartment. Note also how many subcultural activities take some space, and out in the suburbs is where such space is. Active leisure activities and single-house living came in together.

A short walk in any suburb, plus reading a few notices scattered around on supermarket bulletin boards, in newspapers, and similar locations, will suggest the extent of the avocation subcultures. As far as I know, no one has ever even tried to categorize the kinds of things people do, often with great intensity and skill, but it would make an interesting list. One complete set deals with autos and other engine-powered stuff—this group includes hot rodders, antique and special-interest car buffs, specific-make clubs (e.g., the MG fans), motocycle groups (subdivided in endless ways), funny-car fans, snowmobile users, touring groups, motor-scooter types, and many others.

Another group deals with crafts, ranging from wood-work and pottery-making to home repair to machine-shop and welding practice. This group often blends with the artistic types—the fellow who welds car frames for fun becomes the sculptor who makes interesting steel-rodded shapes. Then there are the music fans. (This group has benefited enormously from really good repro-ductive techniques on records and tapes); the amateur theatrical bunch; photographers; the readers and biblio-philes; and the collectors of just about everything, from stamps to bottles to Mickey Mouse watches. The antique and art collectors fit in this group as well.

Travelers and outdoorsmen (including fishermen of all types, campers, hunters, hikers, and bike riders) are a huge group. They tend to be very visible on the high-ways, since their campers, boat trailers, and vans are moved along them. They also potentially interfere with other groups, and there is always debate among the National Rifleman's Association, the Sierra Club, and all the rest.

The surprising part about this list of avocations, incomplete as it is, is that most of these activities were either small or nonexistent even thirty years ago. A few wealthy collectors had stamps, antiques always were picked up by someone, and farmer-hunters are as old as the Republic, but for the typical man (say, not in the top 5 percent in income terms), such hobbies and handicrafts simply did not exist. Men worked too hard and had too little time or money to fool around. But our middle American of today has more options to use up his leisure time than anyone could use in five life times. Presumably, he will do what he enjoys—which is the freedom component of avocations. People have nearly absolute freedom to do any variety of things.

Self-selection is easy—you just stumble onto, or deliberately go out and find, people doing the same thing. One curious dimension of a leisure activity is that the people now doing it quickly sense that a newcomer is really interested, and he is welcome. The idle, curious onlookers are sorted out, but the potentially active doer is easily and quickly brought into the game. The procedure is quite democratic and typically follows quite precise, yet unwritten rules. Consider one subculture inhabited by around 130,000 adult Americans: model railroading. To the outsider, mention of model trains resurrects images of Lionel toys around the Christmas tree years ago. An adult who is involved with such things is bound to be a bit peculiar. But if you happen to really like the idea of building your own model trains, the information system on how to participate is wide open. Just wander down to the nearest modestly large magazine stand and pay seventy-five cents for the latest copy of *The Model Railroader* or *Model Craftsmen*. The outsider, flip-

ping the pages, will see excellent photos of and articles
about models which clearly are not toys—what are they?
Reading more closely, you will note articles with incomprehensible titles such as "Gaps and Feeders in Blind
Faith," or "Traub's Wheel Collett." And there are ads
like no mass circulation magazine ever saw, full of facts,
not puffery. Try this for superlative ad prose:

> Reverse-loop direction switch. A built in electrical
> feature which eliminates complex external connec-
> tions when you are wiring turning tracks. Of course
> [the] 602 also has main line direction switch.

Whoever's buying is not exactly going to be emotion-
ally turned on!

If the casual reader likes to probe further, he can find
the hobby shop and club directories for the whole nation
(and some foreign countries) listed in the magazine. And
if he gets carried away and drops in to the nearest hobby
shop, he may spend an hour or two chatting with the
proprietor, who is perhaps more interested in showing
him what it's all about than in making a sale. The shop-
owner will be pretty knowledgeable too, or he won't be
in business long. If the newcomer goes down to a local
model-railroad club, he will typically find the place half
torn-up, with lots of presumably serious men working
very hard on very little. But they will psych out the newcomer, find out if he's just curious or seriously interested, within twenty minutes. If he's interested, welcome
to the club, literally! The boys will be friendly, and within
an hour the newcomer is likely to be painting something.
If he gets hooked, the old hands will be more than happy
to show him how it's all done.

Since 130,000 guys each spending two or three hundred dollars a year are of interest to manufacturers and
advertisers, there have even been some market studies of

the types of people who are model railroaders. They tend to be serious, quite well-educated people in their thirties, with better than average jobs—but rarely at the top. Apparently, many of them get their satisfaction avocationally, not vocationally. And, apart from an occasional public exhibition, no one ever heard of this crew. They go merrily along, admiring their heroes (the fellows who regularly have their home layouts written up and photographed in the magazines, or who are known to produce great craftsmanship), build things like 1936 Norfolk and Western mallets, and generally have a ball. If their wives can learn to tolerate their idiosyncrasies, they make the best husbands around. Once you get married and get a house with a big basement for your railroad layout, nothing so trivial as a domestic quarrel will ever get you out of there. Railroaders' wives always know where they are, and many wives join in, too.

And indeed, quite unnoticed by anyone else, these fellows produce some awfully good art, both in equipment and scenery. The best model railroads are not perfect representations of reality in 1/87th the size of the real ones, but much more. They are reality as seen from a peculiar perspective, which only the in group really recognizes. A fellow like the late John Allen, of Monterey, California, was one of this generation's really great artists, but few outside the fraternity have ever heard of him. Indeed, few model railroaders know what he did for a living—it didn't really matter to them. They do know he created some of the best sculpture in the world, and it was all for fun.

Here are a bunch of presumably sane, serious citizens, who have self-selected themselves into a specific group. The purpose of the group is to have fun, and presumably they do. They are willing to spend their time and money on this hobby, and many of them find real satisfaction, more than on any job, in this avocation. Model railroad-

ers are harmless; they don't bother anyone, ever—but
their avocation gives them a new and often extremely
rich dimension to their lives.

Avocational activities give participants, particularly
those who become officers of the group, status. The
president of the local model-railroad club may be a quiet,
unassuming follower on the job, but in his avocation, he
is an important man. He is responsible for a whole series
of complex tasks, including real estate deals (to get space
for club operations), organizing meetings and shows,
finding funds, and all the other things which need to get
done. Many persons who would never be close to the top
in any conventional work or even leisure situation become very effective administrators and managers when
they take over club responsibilities. It's no surprise that
such activities can be very important to the individuals
involved. For many decades we have been bemused by
the head of the church ladies' aid society, but we often
forget that there are thousands of other, low-profile organizations of every type, with each one needing its
president, secretary, and treasurer. For many people,
such positions are more important than anything they do
at their job.

This freedom explosion in doing your avocational
thing is so recent that few have yet even thought about
its implications. One key point is that having lots of
widely varied avocations around means that people, as
usual, have more options. What they select may seem
crazy to others, but it is very important to the participants. These activities lock into other parts of the private
life, like having cars to get to distant meetings, being able
to afford the odds and ends that any avocation requires,
and having enough time to do the job. And the groups
tend to be very democratic and brotherly. They accept
you for what you are, no matter what that is. Model
railroaders don't argue politics—that's outside the

game. Neither do chamber-music groups. As long as you observe the unwritten ethical codes of the insiders, no one bothers you, and indeed, you are a friend. And when you are a friend, you get invitied to other houses, eat together, travel together, and all the rest, because you are one of the chosen. Since anyone can be in any group whose rules he is willing to observe, this is real freedom. It also is freedom in another dimension—no one has to join or do anything. If you don't want to play, no one will make you.

The best guess for 1984 is that such avocational options will continue to expand. Every year some subculture pops up, doing something new that had not been thought of before. People seem willing to spend their time and their money on things they enjoy. They have the time; increasingly they have the money—so why not? The implications for society are worth thinking about.

# 8

## ■ ■

# *Automobiles*

The auto is the enemy of society—and all that is sound and pure and good. Consider the evidence: the auto kills at a faster rate than all wars put together, to say nothing of injuring millions. In 1970, 55,300 people were killed in traffic accidents of all sorts, while an almost unbelievable 5.1 million were injured by the monsters. If one is interested in lethal instruments in our society, nothing Americans do comes even remotely close to being as deadly as riding in an ordinary automobile.

Autos also pollute, as anyone who has tried to breathe what is laughingly called air in Los Angeles knows full well. The list of deadly fumes, poisons, and noxious substances which they create and which are clearly hazardous to health is long. And if one tosses in traffic congestion and noise pollution, it is clear that autos are a major contributor to the unhappiness of virtually all Americans. Autos are also notorious space-eaters, using up open land for roads, parking, garages, and streets at a fantastic rate. Freeways through cities have long been the best slum-clearance projects we have—they quickly chew up square blocks of everything. And families owning cars need multiple space, at times more for the car and related sundries than for living quarters.

Cars also use up scarce natural resources, including irreplaceable ones such as petroleum. The pollution created by making the steel, rubber, fibers, and other products used to make the cars is also extreme—to say nothing of the waste and pollution caused by discarding some six to seven million cars per year. And cars also generate various service baronies to serve them, in auto manufacturing companies, petroleum refining, and maybe worst of all, in highway departments, who seem often to consist entirely of philistines whose only interest is tearing out everything esthetic and useful to create yet more acres of concrete for the monsters to drive on. Such public agencies seem out of control, loaded with cash from fuel and use taxes, totally indifferent to any problem aside from their own narrow road-building interests.

Cars also change health and morals, probably for the worse. People drive instead of walking or riding bicycles, and they get heart disease. Some people even use cars to commit suicide. And with a car, young people can get off the front porch and out someplace alone—and who knows what happens then? Young people discovered this before 1920, and enthusiastically took up motoring. Older people still worry, and they should—a surprisingly high percentage of living Americans were probably conceived in an automobile.* Cars are also in their pres-

---

*Motor Trend* recently and nostalgically pointed out that auto lovemaking is undoubtedly on the decline. It is hard to make love in a modern 2 by 2 sports car, and young people are a lot more affluent these days than they used to be, so motels and apartments are more important. But they undoubtedly get to those pads by driving.

ent form not viable in the long run. By the year 2000, we will have run out of petroleum, polluted absolutely everything, and generally wrecked the world.

And, finally, it is clear that autos interfere with the rights of others in a very significant manner. Nondrivers have to breathe too; people wanting to ride buses find none, because there are not enough nondrivers left to finance the system; bicyclists can't find room on the roads; pedestrians are among the casualities; and anyone living near a major road has plenty of noise and air pollution to fight, like it or not. Given this list of maladies, it is hard to figure out what more antisocial instrument could have been invented if you sat down and tried hard.

But after all is said and done, we like autos. Americans buy eight to ten million new cars a year; drive them more each year; and generally accept them as an integral part of their lives. Minor efforts at banning cars (as in putting in a pedestrian mall instead of a street downtown) have not produced good results. The malls look good, and they attract a few people for a while, but most people return to the shopping center, where they can park. Indeed, they go off in their cars to do everything—ride to work, take vacations, bank, see movies, transport the kids to school, or just mess around. One of the surest forecasts anyone can make is that the total number of passenger miles generated by cars will rise next year in the United States. Except for World Wars I and II, and the depth of the Depression year 1932, this number has gone up three to ten percent per year ever since 1900. There is no indication that it will fall in the foreseeable future.

So a country of 206 million people has 88.8 million cars, along with 17.9 million trucks and buses. Eighty-two percent of the 63.7 million families in the country own a car, and 29 percent of these families have two or more. There is enough automotive capacity to give everyone in the country a ride in the front seat at once, even without crowding. As long ago as 1928, there was one car for every five people in the United States. The simple truth is we like cars. Why? Well, it gets back to personal freedom. Granted that the auto is everything its critics say, it is also freedom for the common man. We buy them and adjust to them because they give us great personal flexibility.

It is no accident that real freedom for a young person begins when he finally gets his driver's license. For the first time in his life, he can go where *he* wants, not where someone else wants. He can take anyone *he* wants to wherever they want to go, whenever *he* wants to go. All that's needed is the money to buy the car, pay the license taxes, get some insurance, and purchase the fuel. If you can do this, you are free, in a way no one outside the twentieth century could ever really grasp. Understand this, and it is easy to see why most people chose to own cars.

Cars are complex machines, but not so complex that a reasonably bright teen-ager cannot mess around inside them and figure out what's wrong, which is no small thing in our anonymous society. Cars give you freedom from the tyranny of bus and train schedules as well. Those who urge us to take the train fail to mention the inevitable strike. If you have a car, to hell with the strikers. The railroad advocates also fail to note that cars give the freedom of selective privacy, where you can enjoy the decor and interior, along with the radio, air conditioning, or hi-fi that *you* want, when *you* want it. You also get to be with *your* friends, not a bunch of characters who happen to be on the train. It is no accident that the organizations who want the very best personnel always seem to be in (or about to move to) some location which is convenient to get to by car.

A car provides incredible flexibility. If you're looking for a job, you can go a long way; if you're taking a vacation, you can go wherever you want; if you just need to run down to the store to pick up a forgotten item, you can go. No other form of transport (except in some few cases, your feet, a motorcycle or a bicycle, all equally personal forms) can match it.

Curiously, cars are cheaper than most forms of transport. Average total costs per mile for American cars are around twelve or thirteen cents these days, as compared to four to six cents by bus or train, and up to seven cents by air. If you have three people in a car, per passenger costs are lower than any public transport. And if you get five people in your car, your operating costs are so low that it's the cheapest way you can get anywhere. The reason is that roads are rented through the gas tax, and with 108 million other cars and trucks paying their share, it is very cheap for any one car to use a good road at any time. Moreover, the driver doesn't pay himself to drive, and in a high-labor-cost economy, this factor is very significant in reducing costs. Actually, most of the time the driver is having fun. A surprisingly large number of people do like to drive, even in congested commuter conditions.

Among other things, a car is an ego builder. Where else in this world can the common man or woman casually command three hundred horsepower so easily? Cars are extensions of ourselves, a way of showing the world what we really are. Big ones, little ones, economy or show, plush or Spartan, hotted up or small four-cylinder jobs—they all tell the world what kind of person we wish we were.

Autos snuck up on us, which is one reason why it is hard to think straight about them. In 1900, they were cute toys for the rich; by the 1920s they were essential items for most of us. They hit us too hard too soon for anyone to figure out what was really going on, so we wallow around in various control philosophies, not ever sure of what to do about them. And our thinking about cars suggests that we still don't quite know how to get a handle on the problem.

Many planners and social philosophers are bothered by cars, given all the problems they have. But too often it is assumed that all those people out there are irrational, while the planners are sober, rational, and serious. No so—the key lies in considering the personal freedom implications of cars. The carless person becomes a slave to a rapid transit line, the air transport system, his own feet, or the trains and buses. A planner knows all about him, where he can go and when. And that *is* power. It is no accident that Communist states are very dubious about cars—if the leaders are to lead, the last thing they want to do is give any person a way to escape their control.

Planners attitudes toward cars may also be one major reason why Americans don't really trust the government any more. What the average guy wants is better roads, better cars, and fewer taxes. Even the dimmest-witted citizen these days realizes that these desires are supposedly antisocial, so most of them don't push very hard. What does the government want? Get the cars out of here, that's what! And at this point, the citizens turn off. Hard-nosed local politicians rarely, if ever, try to ban cars or cut the roads and streets budget. They know that if they did, out they would go. It would be fun to have them try, and see if their perceptions are correct.

Actually, though it talks a lot, the government rarely really tries to control cars and drivers. This comment seems strange, given all the safety and antipollution laws which have come along in the past ten years, to say nothing of the more extensive controls and increased emphasis on safe-highway design. But, as we shall see, if anyone were really serious about controlling cars, more could be done than has been done.

So what will we have in 1984? There are two major options. One would involve taking to heart the anti-auto philosophy and beginning to cut back on auto use. The other option would involve slowly trying to learn to live with the beasts.

Getting rid of cars has two drawbacks: first, you would have to restructure American life back to 1910 spatially, economically, and vocationally; and second, no one can figure out the politics of the problem, given the American love affair with the car. As we suggested earlier, if you banned cars from the cities, the cities would go, not the cars. And it is hard to figure out how to run businesses, get to work, shop, go to school, or whatever, with the population spread around like it is, without using cars.

Another major problem is what to do about the millions of jobs which relate to cars—filling stations, repairs, gadgets, road building, construction, and all that. One suspects that these people could eventually be reemployed but our present and past experience in getting rid of well-entrenched interests (like the military) gives one pause. A couple of million respectable, enraged voters can be an awesome force.

But suppose that sometime between now and 1984, we do begin to cut back sharply on auto use. What kind of world will we have? Presumably there would be a return to cities, since we would need to get back close together without auto transportation, and the advantages of spreading out would be lost. One could forecast a great high-rise apartment boom, along the new rapid transit lines. Railroads would be in great shape, as trucks were eliminated; mass transit and bus companies might even become growth industries again. One would also expect a boom in other kinds of enterprises and government agencies which provide public goods and services, such as city parks, police protection, and museums.

Actually, we know all about such a world—it existed, in a lively way, in any American city around 1930. Cars were there, but they were relatively few, being rationed by their high price. (They were too expensive for the average workingman.) Streetcars and buses were doing good business in all cities, and apartment and flat living was the way of life for most people. A few rich folk lived in the suburbs, but they were not the mainstream of America. The railroads handled over 90 percent of inter-city shipments. And people were even happy.

You can also see this same world right now in any developed Communist country. Go to Moscow, to Warsaw, to Prague, and it's all there. The reason is that Communist rulers have never provided the cars, electric energy, multiple-channel TV programming, and other freedom instruments which Americans take for granted. And because they have not, their cities look just about like ours did in 1930. They even lack the outdoors, flashy display advertising which we find so disturbing, but for different reasons. We didn't have much of this in 1930 because no one knew about neon tubing. The Communists restrict this kind of advertising for ideological reasons.

You can walk the grim, gray streets of any Communist city and see what ours would look like if we did what many are now suggesting we do about cars. Life would be quiet, sedate, and much simpler. No one would collect his antiques or butterfles because he could not drive to where they are, nor would he have the necessary display space to put them in his crowded apartment. No one would go out to Montana to camp, because he could not get there from here.

Because lots of us have tasted automotive sin, getting from where we are to this new carless world would present some problems. A common error in discussing massive social controls is to assume control costs are zero. If we sharply limited car use, can we assume that everyone would sigh and obey the regulations? Since some cars will have to be permitted, the most common reaction will be, "How do I get a permit?" A few million owners would go to the black market for the permits. Others would besiege the licensing office, trying to work out an angle. So we would need lots of new policemen to control the situation and still more people to run the licensing office. The name of the game would be to obtain real status by obtaining auto permits, just as the name of the game in the past forty years has been to get a car by earning enough money to buy one.

Situations where permits and rationing are used to control scarce things lead to the smart guys winning. The not so smart lose. The hustler who really reads the permit law and finds in paragraph 9 (c) some excuse that just might allow him to have a car, gets one—and the wealthy man who has his lawyer do the same gets his, too. But the poor and ignorant do not. So there would be significant redistribution of convenience in favor of the rich. Incidentally, the Soviets know all about this: The commissars and the other big wheels get cars!

It seems unlikely that a carless world will really come to pass despite the talk. There is just too much pressure for the other kind of mobile world we have. The best guess is that we will learn to live with cars, and make some efforts to control them in acceptable ways. Much can be done, if one begins to think about what is really going on right now.

One thing to do is to do nothing. Presently, urban areas (including the suburbs) take up less than 2 percent of all the land in the U. S. The common accusation that cars eat up space is true, but they eat up space no one really wants. Anyone who has driven the freeway across

Wyoming or Nevada cannot get excited about using up scarce space. If you leave people alone, they tend to find their own best solutions. Those who hate cars find high-density city neighborhoods where they are undisturbed, and where they really don't need cars. Those who love their autos will go to suburbs along a freeway. Even if they are black, chicano, or female, and hence discriminated against, they can find a spot which is adequate, if not utopian.

The strategy of doing nothing grandiose is exactly what we have been doing for the past fifty years. Eighty percent or so of the population took a look at their cars and their life styles, and self-selected themselves into places where they could live with themselves, their neighbors, and their cars. Those who chose opposite courses (or were forced to because they couldn't afford it—most non-car-owning families are very poor) managed to fit themselves into some other pattern.

In the process of apparently doing nothing, actually we have done a great deal to adopt to the car (though not nearly enough). Most of it has been done outside the traditional city. We have built the best highway system in the world, and we annually spend over $15 billion on roads. What we have never done is made any effort to integrate this expenditure with other transport systems, such as jitney transport in cities, or rail freight transport. Americans have historically disliked extensive system-wide planning, and nowhere in American life does this show up so vividly as in transportation. Efforts to move toward more integration have always come to grief on the objections of many vested interests. Now we are beginning to see what the problem is, but it will be a long time before we see any really comprehensive transport planning. Many federal officials have pushed hard for such planning, but various interests have properly suspected that if one group or another is selected to do the planning, the other transport interests will lose. More-over, good planning in transportation is so complicated that no one yet knows how to do it right.

Since a suggestion to do nothing doesn't appeal to Americans, what else could we do? Well, we could improve auto safety. We now have auto-safety laws, plus, perhaps even more significantly, highway-safety design, which get at part of the problem. The *rate* of accidents per 100 million car miles driven has been falling steadily since the 1920s. Better cars, plus well-designed freeways and other road improvements, have done a good job. This is one reason why drivers don't worry too much. A typical driver will see far fewer accidents, and get involved in many fewer, than he would have ten years ago.

What else could we do? We could pay more attention to drivers. Present pressures focus on the car and road. This is politically realistic since safe roads and cars are speedy and comfortable and noncontroversial. Drivers are not. Drivers vote, and often their livelihood depends on their cars, so politicians tread softly. Nevertheless most of us are rather inept amateurs. So although insurance companies and safety experts have long pointed it out, we have ignored the most dangerous part of the car. Half of all serious accidents involve drunken drivers—why not get them off the road? Hard politically, but easy technically—drunks are not all that hard to find.

Another possibility is to figure out how to tell others which drivers may be dangerous. The British have been doing it for years with drivers who are just learning. Learners are required to have big red *L*'s on the car, front and back. Other drivers avoid them like the plague since experienced drivers, knowing a potential danger, act accordingly. We could extend this system with a whole code of license plates, say yellow plates for old ladies with slow reflexes; green ones for really good drivers; and red ones for dangerous people. One state has already proposed a red plate for those convicted of drunken driving. Lack of knowledge can be a very dangerous thing when driving a car, and a way of telling what that nut ahead of you is apt to do could avoid a lot of accidents. The point is that a bit of creative thinking, plus some political maneuvering, can make cars safer than they now are. And not to be forgotten are the ongoing programs to make safer roads and build safer cars.

Pollution is being attacked vigorously by new antipollution laws, led by California, which has very special troubles of its own. So by 1984, when the 1974 cars will be getting old and retired rapidly, there will be much less pollution than there now is. In spite of lots of panic talk, in most places and at most times, auto-caused pollution is not very dangerous. Places with special atmospheric conditions, like Los Angeles, or with very high densities like New York City, have problems, but out in smaller cities and suburbs, to say nothing of the sticks, where most of us are, and more of us will be, it doesn't look too serious. One thing which could be done, if we *really* were worried about pollution would be to have a horsepower tax, along with pollutant taxes. The bigger the car, the higher the tax—because such vehicles use more fuel and pollute more. The more the vehicle pollutes, the higher the tax on its purchase. Such taxes, judiciously applied, would quickly lead to the sale of less polluting vehicles.

We will also see the development of different motive power, which will be less polluting. Use of natural gas is one possibility (ordinary gasoline engines can run on the stuff with minor alterations—but where do you get the natural gas?); steam is another. Turbines, Wankels, and Sterlings are under intensive experimentation. Electrics offer still another possibility, but until someone figures out better and more efficient batteries (or fuel cells) such vehicles will stay on golf courses and retirement villages. There are also some people studying the use of hydrogen.

Technological development, which is what today's auto needs, is exactly what Americans are very good at. It is like getting to the moon—complex, but basically a problem in applied science and engineering. The human element is minimal. We may be unable to change driving habits, or get people to shift their thinking to include buses, but we know how to solve a technical problem. Actually, this one is easier than getting to the moon, since there is big money in the solution. The company which comes up with a usable, pollution-free, noiseless, safe car will make a mint. Already the big auto companies, and hundreds of little scientifically oriented firms that few have heard of are actively experimenting.

While we are doing all these things to improve the automobile we have got to live with, we might take some small comfort in the fact that things are really not as bad as some people say they are.

Cars *are* space eaters, but we have space to burn in the United States. In the older cities now coming apart, we don't; but they aren't the entire United States. Those living in places designed with cars in mind wonder what the problem is. Incidentally, changing cities may destroy lots of things, some of them nice things, but not the entire Western cultural heritage. Indeed, many of our really great artists, writers, and scientists before 1830 did their work in what we now call suburban conditions, with human instead of electrical energy to run the houses. Maybe geniuses were inspired by serving girls, assorted flunkies, and the laborers who kept the places going, but one suspects not.

As the country steadily gets restructured toward fitting in cars better, more logical and maybe even more esthetic solutions to the parking problem might be found. It is really a question of scale. A few cars stretched along a tree-shaded suburban street, or tucked away in garages, are not objectionable, but when one sees acres of cars on some asphalt lot, they look terrible. If we insist on bringing very large numbers of people together, like at athletic events or in major shopping centers, some visual pollution is inevitable. But if we continue to splatter out around the countryside, the scattered parked cars won't bother anyone. Where such conditions now exist, no one cares. And by 1984, there will be a lot more scattering.

Autos do use up scarce resources but any economist would point out that these are nowhere near scarce enough to make anyone interested in recycling them efficiently. Fuel is still so cheap that we have big cars; and to date, it is cheaper to make them new than to recycle them. In India, laborers cut apart old tires to salvage the wire in the tire beads. In the United States, 250 million worn out tires pile up each year. Recycling old stuff is labor-intensive, which is poison to a high-labor-cost economy. But there are some interesting possibilities, if you don't like the visual pollution caused by six million or more junkers each year. Recent interest in eliminating them has led to considerable technological progress in chewing up and sifting out old car hulks. Many companies are now willing to travel around with portable grinders. The auto-wrecking business is a well-organized free market that no one ever pays any attention to, except scrap dealers so very few know that even modest cost changes could lead to all sorts of recycling. Try these as possibilities:

We might, like Sweden, levy a junk tax on every new car sold. Since every car will eventually be a wreck, make the new buyer carry the cost, and use the funds to pick up, scrap, and sort out the old ones. Fifty dollars per car would yield $500 million a year—enough to get rid of every hulk in the country in a relatively short time. Another method no one ever mentions, since wrecking yards are far beyond the attention of anyone in power, is to demand that new cars be built so they can be taken apart economically. A study of auto junking suggests that some two hundred dollars worth of good iron, steel, plastics, copper, aluminum, remains in an old wreck. But it is worth nothing in a city because the various components cannot be easily separated. To do so is a very expensive labor-intensive job. Now any group of engineers designing new cars can surely figure out how to make the key components so that they can be easily separated. Just one example—auto-salvage steel is of low value because it contains too much copper. The copper, which got in there, comes from the myriad of copper wires used everywhere in a modern car. If the car is designed so that the copper can be taken out very easily, wrecks are suddenly much more valuable to auto wreckers. The reason this doesn't happen is someone designs and builds cars, and someone else takes them apart, ten years later. Put both jobs together and, by 1984, old auto hulks will be so valuable that they won't be abandoned anywhere. Aside from cost, there is no reason we couldn't recycle modern cars indefinitely, making only a handful of key replacement parts. The cars would be as good as new. The amount of steel, copper, etc., necessary to hold the fleet at eighty-eight or ninety million indefinitely would be a mere fraction of what it now is. We did this during World War II, and we could do it again. But we probably won't, because we have a long way to go before major scarcities of basic raw materials occur. When they do, prices of new cars will rise and eventually it will pay to fix old cars instead of building new ones.

Some motor-vehicle and public-road departments *are* virtually beyond public control, and some of these outfits do antisocial things like wreck cities, chop down every tree in sight, and generally mess up the environment. Many of them were totally engineering-oriented until rather recently. Engineers can be functional in the narrow sense of the word. But such baronies are eventually subject to control, if people really care, and some changes are occurring. Pressures from ecology experts and anti-auto groups have led to changes, and more will come. A field called organization theory deals in depth with problems of organizational pressures and changes, and it too is developing rapidly. By 1984, we will know how to control such seemingly impregnable organizations. We may even get them operating in a way that minimizes the unpleasant intrusions of the auto.

In the end, the modern gasoline-powered car will disappear, but not by 1984. Around the turn of the century, we will indeed run out of a few key things, like fuel. Some note that this means autos are doomed, forgetting that there are lots of options yet to be developed. Atomic cars? Ridiculous—just like gas-drive engines in 1880. Electric cars? The central power station will pollute more than the cars do—except that we may have some nonpolluting energy source by then. People like freedom, which means they like cars, and they are willing to pay for them. Hence, in 1984 or 2000 we will still be running around in cars—but not the type we now use. Try driving a 1925 Model-T Ford to see why.

# 9

## ■ ■

# *Electronics, Electricity,*
# *Communications, and Sanitation*

Our 1884 citizen could take advantage of some speed of
light communications. The telegraph was already well
established, and telephones were just coming in. But
radio in a practical consumer form did not appear until
the 1920s, and television only began after 1946. However, TV had been demonstrated in 1929 in crude form,
and predicted long before that. The delay shows that it
takes time to get big, complex communications systems
in place. Indeed, we are today working on lots of things
which are very well understood, yet not totally used, such
as cable TV, pocket electronic-calculators, TV cassette
players, and two-way television telephones. We are just
beginning to realize that when a home has the right kinds
of cables hooked up, virtually any kind of information, in
almost any form, can be cheaply transmitted. What it
boils down to is that anything which can be reduced to
some electronic pulsation, coded for transmission and

uncoded at the other end, can be sent. It isn't exactly easy, but it can be done. Moreover, communication is inevitably cheaper than transportation of either people or information, so the possibilities of tradeoffs get very appealing. Actually we've known about this for 140 years. It was a lot easier to send Morse's first cable telegram than it was to ride a horse from Baltimore to Washington; and it is still a lot easier to sit in your living room and watch a football game on TV than to get yourself out to the stadium. The interesting question is how much farther we go—and we could go a long, long way.

A person who can cheaply communicate with the rest of the world is freer and more flexible than the person who cannot. The key word is "cheap." It doesn't do anyone any good to have a phone, if it takes two weeks' income to make a single call. Very few Americans have ever lived in places where telephones were unavailable. When you do, the costs of not having them have to be seen to be believed. Instead of making a two-minute call, a messenger has to be hired and sent. Time required for the communication goes up to five hours or more, while costs skyrocket. Moreover, information orally transmitted is often more garbled and less usable than it would be when received by phone. We Americans are so locked into a world of instantaneous communication that we cannot imagine what any other world is like.

By 1984, we should see quite logical extensions of already known communications techniques, all of which give people more flexibility and freedom. An obvious one is the extended use of cables to make available more TV programming—even now, because cables are in place, odd cities like Bloomington, Indiana, have more TV channels than many metropolitan areas. The only problem which needs to be solved for cable TV to burgeon is the legal question of who makes the money. CATV is clearly a gravy train, and it also is clearly a monopoly situation, like telephones. Who will get the profits? This is now being argued out by the Federal Communications Commission; various promoters and companies who want franchises; city governments who want a cut; and lots of others.

Also clearly in the state of the arts, and awaiting economic and political development, are cable uses such as instantaneous newspapers printed out in your own home, stock-market quotations, access to library materials, access to technical data, and much, much more. Access to information anywhere in the world is possible, once the system is set up. In most cases, someone already has demonstrated practical working systems of data transmission, but such problems as cost of equipment, legal questions (again, who gets the money, and sometimes, who has the copyright), and lack of knowledge about markets can slow up development.

The cost angle is critical, since things get used *en masse* when costs get down to reasonable levels. Right now, you can buy a TV system which will make tapes from present programming, and you can even buy a few cassette tapes of movies and such. But presently they cost too much. When the system costs $400, and you can get all the tapes you want (either rented or sold outright) for $2.95, then the market will really start moving. Would you believe 1975? It's closer than most people think, and a dozen or more companies are eagerly doing their research and development to get the costs down. It is also true that the imagery will get better. The more real it is, the more we like it. TV is better than radio, as one example, and TV telephones, when we get them, will be better than ordinary telephones. TV cassettes, which already are being sold, will be better than records or tapes carrying sound only—by 1984, an opera buff should be able not only to hear his favorites, but also to see the whole performance in living color, for a price not much greater than a sound tape of the music costs now. If you don't like opera, try football, an old western, or a re-re-rerun of *All in the Family* or *Petticoat Junction.*

Television telephones have been around a long time, but once again, high cost and complexity have kept them mainly in the laboratory. Telephone companies are moving very cautiously on this, perhaps feeling that the market will be small and impact minimal—the same things people were saying about television in 1945. It always is refreshing to take a look at early forecasts about important new freedom instruments to see what key people were saying. In 1945, TV talk was largely technical and relied on radio technology for how audiences might react. Most observers missed all the important points about the technology—which weren't technical at all, but social. The pattern is being repeated right now in discussing TV telephones. They will be expensive; most people don't really want to use them; they won't change things much; and so on. Just wait until they become a mass instrument!

We are also likely to get in fairly common usage by 1984 such presently exotic technology as two-way contact from the home to data banks. An author might wish to converse with some computer or other about eighteenth-century land use in England, or a lawyer preparing a brief may wish to know some precedents in a certain type of case. The author goes to his home computer-console and types (or maybe even speaks) his question about what kinds of deeds and titles were used in Cheshire during the time his novel takes place. There is a slight two-second pause, and then a set of deeds are shown on the console screen. The author asks a few more questions, gets more detailed answers, and then, finding exactly what he wants, pushes the PRINTOUT button. The console spits out the copies of the deeds he needs. The computer can be anywhere, like in the British

Museum in London, while the author is at his home in Monterey, California, near the beach.

The lawyer asks his home console for precedents in his case involving rate-making for a telephone company in Massachusetts. After a minisecond pause, the console screen lights up with reproductions of page after page of relevant citations. When he sees something he wants to include in his brief, the lawyer will have that section printed out. Such things are now possible, but expensive —as costs fall, why not have a computer terminal in your home? At present, such consoles are about one tenth as difficult to operate as they were five or ten years ago. Within another ten years, they may be similar to telephones. Few persons who make a phone call know very much about the intricate and complex technology which makes the call possible. They don't have to. It is enough to know how to dial properly. By 1984, we may well have computers that you can talk to, instead of type at. They already exist—the problems are time, money, and economic feasibility.

Not to be forgotten here is the steady change in computers to extreme complexity on the one hand and simultaneously to extreme simplicity on the other. They are more complex, because they can do things thought impossible even a few years back. Geniuses daily come up with new designs and new applications. But computers are also simpler to use—early computers required highly trained men to give them input and read output (just like the early telegraph system, which needed skilled telegraphers to interpret data). But modern computers are pretty easy to use—third-graders can be taught how in a week. To make them easy to use is a tough job, which is why the new computers are so complex. But for the average man, it *is* easier. And if the things can do you some good, they will get used.

None of these communication technologies is science

fiction—they are around and are being used right now. What forecasting is involved is really economic, in that we are not sure how far or fast costs will fall. The odds are that costs will fall very fast—the cost of computing has been falling by half every four or five years now since 1955, and computations which appeared impossible in 1965 because of high costs are now routine. A color TV set could have been built in 1950 for perhaps $1,000 to $3,000; now we get annoyed if we can't get one for $400 or so in inflated 1973 dollars. Minicomputers to replace comptometers now sell for $100 to $300, which is one-fifth the cost of the old mechanical comptometers, and by 1984 they will be still cheaper. In electronics, things always seem to get smaller (often much smaller) and cheaper each year.

The basic reason lies in the whole transistor revolution, which started in 1950. At that time, expensive and power-gobbling vacuum tubes were the only things around to do electronic jobs. Predictions as late as 1955 that even a modest-sized computer would take the Empire State building to house it and Niagara Falls to cool it were based on the fantastic number of vacuum tubes which would be required. But a transistor and all its relatives (diodes, resistors, integrated minicircuits, etc.) have two intriguing characteristics: they are nothing more than small chips of slightly impure elements, which means that they can be very small; and they use very little electric power to operate, which means that they don't generate much heat. And for cost saving, their production can be automated in quite elegant ways. The hard part is in design and production planning. Once that is done successfully, system costs drop very fast.

Transistors also require very little maintenance, which is nice in high-labor-cost economies like ours. Anyone messing with his dead TV set may disagree, since *some* maintenance is always required, but comparison with earlier electronic devices, with all those tubes always burning out, may suggest that maintenance is indeed dropping. After all, there are no moving parts in most electronic gadgets—and, as we all know, if it moves it breaks, sooner or later.

The final gadget for 1984 is still not yet perfected, but sooner or later it will be. It is some sort of three-dimensional, living-color image transmission, one-way for entertainment and amusement, and later two-way for personal interchange and work. This would be a living, three-dimensional, full-color reproduction. You could call (as by phone) anyone or anything from anywhere. It will be—almost—as if your girl friend or wife were in the room with you; your dear old aunt, halfway around the world, could "arrive" for a brief chat; or you could cook up deals or just talk a while with anyone, anytime, anywhere, for a lot less than the cost of going to where they might be. It's not as far out as it sounds: Three-dimensional living-color images are already here, in the form of laser holographs.

The scenario is intriguing. A busy executive wants to have a conference of his top men scattered around the United States and abroad. He calls a conference at ten on Thursday morning, Eastern Standard Time. At the appointed hour, his colleagues gather in special transmission and receiving rooms wherever they are and sit down. The boss sees each one, in full living color, seated at his table, and each businessman sees all the others too. The meeting goes on, and the interchange, argument, and discussion proceeds as if they all were at the home office. Max, out in Singapore, sketches the new cooling tower he's building, which is giving him so much trouble. Sam, in Memphis, looks at the drawing, shakes his head, and sketches a possible change which might solve the problem. The boss, sitting in a picturesque village he likes in upstate New York, asks both some questions about possible cost increases. Pete, in London, suggests a change which could handle the problem more cheaply. Each of them sees all the others, yet nobody has gone anyplace. If you don't like business conferences, how about those fond memories of that attractive girl you met in Nice just last month, while you were on vacation? You're in Chicago, but just dial her number. Then look, talk, and enjoy, almost as if she were live. Fortunately, telephone jamming techniques will also advance very fast, so no one will have to worry too much about being overheard or overseen.

Don't buy any airline stocks, if such technology really gets going. A lot of businessmen and professionals won't travel quite as much. And don't invest in downtown real estate. Unless the professionals, technicians, and executives happen to *like* to be in downtown, crowded conditions, they won't be. The key factor is that you can string a cable anyplace—which is exactly where people will be —anyplace they like to be. And the better cables are, the more likely they can be where they want to. Even now, great men go where they want, and you find them. A brilliant heart surgeon is where he wants to be; if you need him, you find him. Authors, ad writers, some lawyers, and lots of other good professionals tend to locate in places which please them. By 1984, or maybe 1994, many others will do the same.

Now, toss in the later part of the scenario, which is what happens when each of these men finishes work and goes home. Max, in Singapore, stops in his home and plays a cassette TV tape of *The Marriage of Figaro,* since he's an opera buff. He sinks into his easy chair, and the opera begins, with full hi-fi sound and full three-dimensional color. The boss in upstate New York, always the businessman, goes to his computer terminal and asks for data on the state of the economy. On his screen appear the necessary charts, graphs, and figures he needs, analyzed by top economists and government statisticians. He then asks his broker's office for key data on a couple of hot stocks he thinks may go up, and once again, his screen is filled with relevant data.

Sam says to hell with work. He's a football buff, and he slips into his TV set a cassette of the Rams-Lions game of two weeks ago. How could those guys have lost? When the key play comes up, he replays it a couple of times, and sees how the guard didn't get into position at the critical time. Oh, well, so he lost five bucks to Joe on that game.

Pete, in London, is a bibliophile, so he's busy contacting the library at the London Museum about a peculiar wording in a text of an early Sherlock Holmes mystery he just picked up. It's different from the accepted version, and he finds out, after some conversation with the museum's computer, that his copy is a pirated edition published in America in 1904. It just might be valuable.

As we have been saying, electronics free you by expanding your options. Back in 1973, all of these men would be having a lonely drink in some motel near the head office, worrying about the long flight home the next day. They would be at the mercy of airline schedules, hijackers, missed connections, and time. Now, they can do their own thing.

If the wheels can do it today, so can the common man tomorrow. One suspects that the choice of entertainment might be significantly different, but there sure will be plenty of it. Moreover, don't forget that the poor struggling young student living in Northern Maine, far from any university, can easily tune into the educational channel for Worldwide U., and study economics or math or anything else taught by a really good teacher. The teacher having two-way feedback from his geographically dispersed students can sit anyplace he wants, too, and respond to questions from really interested young people, wherever they are. He gives an exam, the student takes it, and facsimile transmits it to the professor for reading and grading. Then the professor sends it back. Why mess around at high cost on campus, when you can study anywhere, with the best? Facsimile transmission of pictures for newspapers dates back to 1938, but we haven't yet got it into every home. We may, though, and soon.

Electronic monitoring and information transmission of all sorts can replace much transportation and inconvenience. Consider a person who needs some sort of steady or sporadic medical monitoring, such as checking blood pressure, respiration, or heart action. At present, the way we typically do this is to have such a person get to a doctor's office or clinic or hospital, where he or she can be checked. Many times, everything turns out to be fine. The person has traveled, often at considerable cost and inconvenience, for nothing. In 1984, it will be easy enough to have the necessary monitoring equipment in the home. The patient hooks on, turns the system on, and the data is recorded automatically at some hospital center. If all is OK, the relevant doctor is notified in due course. But if it isn't, the doctor is notified immediately so corrective action can be taken.

There is really no particular reason why such monitoring should be done in one place, assuming that we can develop cheap two-way data and information transmission from anyplace—and that is exactly what will happen. Costs for complex computing and informational electronics systems are falling very fast, and as a result, use rates are exploding. By 1984, one can confidently expect that today's applications will look very simple indeed.

And by 1984, or maybe 1994, we won't need a post office. You will write to anyone you want, and the message can be transmitted immediately to him or her. Each house could have a receiver console, perhaps hooked up through the cable for TV, or maybe the phone. When you write your letter, you punch your friend or colleague's number, put the letter in your slot, and it gets reproduced at the other end immediately. It would be a lot easier to transmit coded electronic pulses, decode them, route them, and print them out, than to ship around little pieces of paper. Companies have known this for a long time and use telex and other teleprinters. Only costs and lack of interest have kept such innovations out of the home. The typical modern teleprinter is a big mechanical gadget with lots of maintenance—we need (and will get shortly) totally electronic machines which will do the job faster and cheaper.

Because electronic devices don't use much electric power, and because they don't normally interfere with others, there is little static about using them. But they are time bombs for destroying cities and altering our present way of life. If we eventually build up a complete cable net, with connections to every home and organization (we already have, with the telephone—it took eighty years. Perhaps we can finish the rest of the job in less time), then anyone can live anywhere. And he probably will. A surprising amount of what we call work could just as easily be done at home as at the office, assuming that each worker could contact anyone he wanted, anytime he wanted, in the way he wanted—which often would involve watching the person's face as he talked. We get a large amount of good feedback this way, which is why so many kinds of things are done personally, such as deal cooking, technical discussion, and teaching. Actors and teachers can tell you that there is a profound difference between being on television, with only that cold-eyed camera on you, and working in front of a live audience. To date, we just don't know enough about how two-way TV would work to know if the feedback would be adequate for everyday use. But such systems would probably cut out an awful lot of transportation to assure interpersonal contact. By 1984, we will know, and it is likely that it will be all bad news for cities and good news for everyone else.

So, we put the pieces together, and what do we have? A man sits in his house, tied into the world by his electronic gadgets and his electric power, his car outside ready to take him anyplace he wants when he wants. Increasingly a man's home is his castle, with a bunch of electronic and electrical slaves to do all the work. The isolation can be complete, if you want it that way, or you can stick your castle in a flat in Manhattan. Location increasingly doesn't matter, so, be where you want to be. You may still be tied into the job at the plant or office, so you locate within twenty or thirty miles of it. Your kids may want personal contacts, and maybe you do too, so you avoid remote mountaintops and settle for single-family housing in some suburb or another. Whatever you decide is your business. You do what when you want to, and you can link into anything that interests you whenever you please. And that *is* freedom.

Note that historically, the only way to enjoy this type of freedom was to be stinking rich and powerful—you had to control the peasants so that they would do the dirty work for you and you needed lots of land to grow forage for your work animals. If you weren't quite so rich, you had to live close in to be close to your job, amusements, and general labor sources, such as laundries and cleaners and watchmakers. Your transport system was so inadequate that you had to be either close to a streetcar line or some other form of mass transportation. Now, none of these old constraints apply. You are more free, and you are also more dispersed. Things that used to get done in person are now done electronically. All of this snuck up on us, and few even realize how much trading off we do between communications and transportation. But we do trade off because it happens to be convenient, and we will continue to do it more in the future.

With the new communications, older people win big, because the older you are, the harder it is to transport instead of communicate. TV was a great gift to the old, as phones were, because they both enable oldsters to get in on the world without moving around so much. The young, who still want to get around nonselectively and find out what the world is about, benefit less. Historically, you went downtown to do this, but downtown in its older form isn't there anymore. Perhaps this is yet one more reason for the generation gap—the older folks above thirty are living an isolated life style which the young find rather incomprehensible. But with a bit of luck, we may even evolve new forms of interpersonal contact which will help the young. We already have, for a lot of younger people—it's called a college, and that's one major reason why colleges are so popular. The young can get together there for *their* things in a socially accepted way. Not that the young don't eagerly lock into the parts of the system that appeal to them. One of the first freedom instruments a ten-year-old learns to use is the telephone, and TV watching is a way of life even before that. When a youngster can call his girl on a TV telephone, he will love that, too.

While some persons in the family are watching the video cassettes, studying by remote control, or whatever, the house has to be run too. And since no one has servants of the human type any more, we have to have other kinds. The place is being heated or cooled by gas, oil, or electricity; the clothes are in the automatic washer, or maybe in the electric or gas dryer; the housewife disposes of the garbage with an electric crusher and makes coffee with an electric coffee maker. She is cleaning her oven with ultrasonic sound, generated electrically, and so it goes. No science fiction here—this equipment has been around for a long time, like since the 1920s or 1930s. The only new thing is how pervasive it is. Only a rich housewife could have had a Bendix automatic washer in 1939; now most families do.

Not to be forgotten, although it usually is, is the home-craft trend so many Americans appear to be on. The sales of such power tools as quarter-inch electric drills, jigsaws, bench saws, lathes, sanders, and all the rest is huge and growing. It is surprising how many Americans seem to be able to do things around the house they couldn't do before, like fix the plumbing, make some shelves, or repair electric circuits. I've seen a complete replica 1910 Ford body made entirely in a home garage by a hobby craftsman, using only his own power and hand tools—in 1910, it took every individual skill the society had to produce that item, and now an amateur can do it better.

To get all this done, you have to be tied into the electric mains, and over 95 percent of American homes are. Electric energy, so far, is cheap energy, and it is noiseless, odorless, and nonpolluting at the point of use. No wonder people enjoy it so much, and so many manufacturers eagerly invent new gadgets to use it. This has been so successful in the past thirty years that now we have an energy crisis, because we can't expand our electrical output fast enough.

Electricity is nonpolluting at the using end, but back at the power plant, there is pollution all over the place. Burning coal or any other hydrocarbon causes it, while atomic-fission plants present the danger of radioactive poisoning. Anyone near the plant will object, which sometimes means that they don't get built, or they get delayed. Moreover, in many parts of the country, there isn't enough clean fuel to burn to make power. So, as we get into the 1970s, we hear forecasts of absolute energy shortages, inability to supply enough natural gas (which is delightfully clean-burning); and potential disaster.

In the end the compound upward curve of energy production will run out, though not by 1984. By 1984, we will be in very short supply of cheap, clean energy sources, since energy use will have doubled by that time. Natural gas, one of the really clean and historically cheap fuels to use, already is being rationed to new users. There is just not enough around the United States.

Two key facts will save us, however. One is that in the *world* there is enough hydrocarbon energy available to keep us going for fifty years or more. Most of it is in the Middle East, and the United States has restricted imports since 1958, to protect local supplies. Now that the local supplies are overtaxed, we will try to buy more abroad, regardless of political risks. The second key fact is that there is enough *raw* energy in the solar system to last us for millions of years. Such power sources as hydrogen fusion, sunlight, the earth's internal heat, tidal energy, windpower, waterpower, and maybe even harnessing of gravitational attraction are all known and all enormous.

The problem is how to use the energy. Down the road, and probably just beginning around 1984, is clean, non-polluting energy. It may come in the form of hydrogen fusion—already there are signs of key breakthroughs, and if they occur, we will have enough energy to do what we want for a millenium and longer. Perhaps tidal power will look more attractive, as costs of natural gas and petroleum rise; solar power in the form of huge reflecting mirrors in our deserts is also a real possibility. We may even burn hydrogen gas instead of natural gas in our home furnaces, and maybe in our cars too. This gas, which is the most abundant element on earth, burns to water and is totally nonpolluting. If we could figure out how to separate it from water cheaply, our problems would be solved. Using geysers and volcanic heat to gen-

erate electric power through steam turbines is a very old
science, but so far we have only tapped the obvious
sources.

Energy sources which do not involve petroleum are
likely to be explored much more exhaustively and
quickly than they have been in the past, because we no
longer have cheap sources of petroleum. And as costs
rise, interest in substitutes also rises rapidly. Moreover,
foreigners, aware that they hold the key petroleum supplies, are likely to be much harder bargainers than they
used to be when the United States had its own supplies.

Not to be forgotten is the old standby, coal. Our present energy crisis has been termed a sulphur crisis, because much American coal has a high sulphur content. It
cannot be burned in power stations without expensive
desulphurization and cleaning. But cleaning is becoming
more attractive as alternative fuel costs rise. Also, coal
can be gassified and used in place of natural gas (at costs
which aren't much higher than present natural-gas
prices), and it also can be made into synthetic gasoline.
And if we insist on driving gasoline-powered cars, the oil
shales in Utah contain enough fuel to last a long time—
if we want to strip-mine isolated areas and make the
necessary plant investments.

The odds are very good that by 1984 we will be well
on our way to resolving our energy crisis. It may also be
that as some kinds of energies get more expensive, we
may stop using them in wasteful ways. If aluminum gets
expensive because making it uses so much energy in the
form of electric power, then less aluminum and more of
some other metal will be used. Scrap supplies also would
be much more carefully gathered than now, as prices
rise. We often tend to assume that something now being
used will continue to get used, *regardless of what it costs.*
Hence, in the 1880s, it was obvious to any serious citizen
that billiards would always be a game for the rich, since

any idiot could calculate the supply of ivory available and determine that only a small number of balls could ever be made.

Fuel cells are one development which show promise in being able to generate large amounts of energy in small packages. They have been used in all our space-exploration work, and experimentally on a few buildings here and there, but like many other things they are just too expensive for home use. But with some luck and hard work, the costs may fall. The average citizen can then say good-bye to his friendly local power company. Note that if you generate your own power, you are free to live in the remotest corners of the earth. You can stick your house in a million places that are not served by power lines, marching along poles. Like the other freedom instruments, electricity frees anyone from someone else's control, both locationally and in terms of reliance. If you do your own clothes, when the laundry goes broke or on strike, it doesn't matter. If the plumber's union hikes wages out of sight, you fix the pipes yourself with your electric power tools. It's no accident that we have required electric, phone, gas and other public utilities to serve *all* customers—they would ruin us if they could pick and choose. And in the future, we may just break away from them still further, if we can rely more on ourselves, say with a single home-fuel cell or power pack.

What goes in, comes out, and our more or less happy family taking baths, opening cans, or going to the toilet, uses incredible amounts of water. We can pinpoint the exact moment when this trend began, in 1884, when Sir Thomas Crapper demonstrated his first automatic valve-flush toilet in London. We have tinkered with his invention for a long time, but modern toilets are essentially the same as his ingenious device. Sir Thomas lived in London, a city which had not only a horrendous sewer problem, but lots of water. One wonders what such an inventive man might have come up with if he had lived in arid New Mexico.

Since we need lots of water for toilets, we might as well use lots of it for other things, such as washing clothes, taking baths, doing the dishes, and disposing of garbage. Because our early industrialization efforts took place in soggy locations like the eastern United States, it has rarely occurred to anyone that something else might be used. Hence we all have very large supplies of water run into our homes, and water mains, wells, cesspools, and other related items take up lots of time for citizens, firms, and local governments.

If you assume the now very low price of water will always be low, no matter what happens, and if you assume that there is no feasible way of handling sewage except with water, you can also assume safely that doom is at hand. Just run out the water use curve to 1984, and you will discover that there is not enough water to go around. Hence we all die of thirst on June 4, 1984. Fortunately, there is no reason why water has to stay cheap, and it probably won't as it gets harder and harder to supply in the right places. And there does not seem to be any real reason why we have to use most of the water to bathe, flush toilets, and clean sinks. How about ultrasonic cleaning of people and dishes? It is done now with machine parts. How about some form of toilet that uses chemicals or a very small amount of water? They now exist in mobile house-trailers and small boats, but are not in household use. If you are a potential inventor and promoter, you could do much worse than figure out an economic sewer system which does not use water. Right now, many rural and suburban areas all over the country cannot be built on because soil or rock conditions are not right for water, and hence sewer, drainage. Maybe, by 1984, we will have a dry sewer system—and as much excellent scenic land suddenly becomes feasible for use, there will be even larger suburban and rural growth.

Sewers and water are but one part of the garbage problem. Even if we solve this one, there remains the problem of solid wastes. Although we already have various forms of garbage-compacting machines for home use, which you can see at many department stores, we need something still more useful, such as a gadget that compacts ordinary garbage into useful items, like building bricks. We already have prototypes of such machines —by 1984, we may have a home version.

It is a bit awkward to have huge fleets of sanitation trucks everywhere, going around in a labor-intensive way and picking up all the solid wastes. Certainly we could do better than this—for an investment of a hundred dollars per house, in some type of disposal, we could afford to give every home one—if it got rid of the garbage trucks, men, and landfills. Science-fiction types can dream of some sort of atomic disintegrator, which in the process generates enough electric power to run the house.

The sanitation area is ripe for revolution, because any change for the better means increased freedom. We may escape the city to the suburb and farm, but today we are still prisoners of our sanitation system and the electric-power and water companies. Now, take economic fuel cells, or some other household-size electric-power generator, add a nonwater-intensive sewage system, and toss in a really good garbage compactor, disposal, or whatever. Where can you live? The answer is just about anywhere.

Note also what this revolution will do to land values. A well-developed suburban lot these days, complete with electric-power poles, paved streets, a gas line, a sewer line, and the telephone lines, costs perhaps ten to thirty thousand dollars per acre, and up. Not two miles away, raw land accessible by road, but lacking all other utilities, costs two to six hundred dollars per acre. All we will need, in 1984, is the one line which carries in CATV, plus the telephone line, and we're home free. Guess where lots of people will go.

We see all of these electronic and electrical items all the time, along with new forms of liquid- and solid-waste disposal, either as demonstrations on TV or maybe in an article in a magazine or Sunday paper. And the usual stress is on how ingenious the technology is. Gee, look what the engineers came up with this time! It's the same, only more so.

But it isn't the same. What we are just beginning to see is that all these electronic and electrical tools have a habit of restructuring our whole lives. The place we live, the things we do in the home, the work we do, the way we amuse ourselves, the tradeoffs we make between communication and transportation, and even the way we handle our young—all of these, and many more, are changed by those gadgets. We become different—and we have more options. We also, because of all the electrical slaves, work physically a lot less hard than we used to. Whatever else it is, the real world of 1984 will not be the same, only more so. As things now around get used more widely, and as new electronic and electrical gadgetry gets put into place, what we are as humans will also change. In short, we will be freer than any group has ever been before, which is surely nice to look forward to.

# 10

■ ■

# *The Minorities:*
# *The Young, the Old, and the Losers*

Any older person watching the under-twenty-five-year-olds cavort around can be easily convinced that they are strange people indeed. They insist on weird hair and dress styles, odd social habits, and other behavioral characteristics that are enough to turn off anyone over thirty-five. And perhaps because they grew up with modern information systems, they know how to use them better than their elders, which merely spreads the word even more widely. It would be a backward American indeed who was not aware of the antics of the young.

In large part, this is because there are so many of them. The postwar baby boom peaked in 1961 in terms of total births, so right now there are more young people around then there were when today's over-forty set were young. They jam schools, flood the job market, and generally raise hell. Vietnam demonstrations, college riots, a sky-rocketing crime rate among the young, and perhaps even more sexual permissiveness caused by the pill make everyone nervous. Clearly these young are not quite the same kinds of young that we used to see, and the world is going to be very different later as a result.

Today's young are really the first generation who had it all—telephones, television, cars, electricity, airplanes, the whole works, for all their lives. People over forty can remember the first TV set they ever had, and the difference it made in their lives. If they grew up on farms, they can remember when the REA first brought electric power to the family farm. The young now have had the new freedom-generating instruments all their lives, so they take them all for granted. Today is the way the world always was—history is irrelevant (as it always has been for the young), but this time around it is *really* irrelevant. Those older folks over thirty got programmed differently because they didn't have what really counts.

So the young are different, in ways few older Americans really realize, which is why they merit special attention. It is worth remembering that all who will be adults in 1984 have already been born. Perhaps we can look around and see what a present twenty-year-old will be like when he, too, is over thirty.

A whole set of special structural problems apply largely to the young, and they in large part determine why young Americans behave the way they do. These constraints are largely constraints on young people, and they make the needs of the young quite different. The young, contrary to general opinion, are the most tightly structured people in our society. Few people under eighteen have any economic self-sufficiency; they are forced to depend on parents for support. And this normally means school, school, and more school. The kids, like it or not, are locked into an annual pattern of semesters, learning what someone else says is important, passing

courses, taking exams, interacting for better or worse
with professional teachers and counselors and princi-
pals. If you don't want to play in this game, you can drop
out at sixteen or so, but you quickly become an unper-
son, in a never-never land where there is no job, no role,
no future. So most kids stick it out, because they have
nothing else to do. If you think that a modern American
high school doesn't have the structure of an old-fashioned prison, you're misinformed. Go down and take a
look. The place runs like an 1890s factory, with rules,
bells, schedules, norms, and all the rest. Kids are stuck
with this for twelve years, from six to eighteen. Of
course, they play the game just like the UAW used to play
it in the 1930s in the auto factories. You push to the edge
of the rules just for the hell of it: if hair is supposed to
be a half inch below the collar, would you believe five
eighths of an inch? The youth can cut classes, even riot
or strike once in a while—but in the end he puts up with
it because it's all he has. And once off duty, a student
encounters rigid limitations of income. His very limited
options become clear. The hi-fi set and records, the
hanging around some joint or another, the experiments
sexually, athletically, and criminally, are as patterned as
a minuet. He watches TV, maybe reads a book he's not
supposed to, or just piddles around. Since teen-agers are
so very peer-conscious, the occasional character who
breaks out of the small number of subcultures available
is thought to be a nut.

And after surviving high school, the kids have more
great choices—go to college for a few years and grow up,
join the Army, or be unemployed. A lucky minority with
uncles in a craft union might get an apprenticeship slot,
and a few others can tighten a bolt or two for Ford or
General Motors, but teen-age unemployment rates routinely run over 15 percent, extraordinarily high when
almost half the kids are not even in the labor market

since they are in school. If you're a black kid in the ghetto, the rates go to over 30 percent. So, off to dear old Siwash, like it or not, where young college instructors despair about ever finding some young girl or fellow who really wants to learn something.

True, colleges are a lot looser than high schools, and the kids may get away from home for the first time, but even in college there is tight structure imposed by someone else. You get the right credits, take the necessary exams, and generally sweat through someone else's world. It doesn't end at quitting time, either—you're locked in every day, every night, all the time. Class ends, but there's that paper to write, and even if you refuse to write it, the thing hangs over you. And the old man threatens to cut off the cash if you don't get a C-plus average, so you plug along, hating it all.

In the end, most young people lack two critical freedom generating instruments—cars and money. Typically, they can't afford the cars until they are over eighteen, or maybe even twenty-two if they go on to college, and until they complete their education, or at least grow up a bit, they haven't got the education or training or experience to generate the earning power which would allow them to be themselves and do their own things. You can see in every town or city a few eighteen-year-olds who do work at Ford and make good money—they have cars and freedom. But young people are smart enough to know that such advantages will pass quickly. The big shot at eighteen with his money and cars will be a sad character seven years later at twenty-five, when he is locked into the assembly line at the same pay (or whatever increases the union can wrangle, which never seem to be enough). The eighteen-year-old starting college knows all about Sam, down the street, who just got his M.B.A. degree at twenty-three and is already making more than the guys out in the plant; he also knows all about Alex, who just finished his bar exams and now makes fifteen thousand a year working for that New York law firm. Maybe, if he can stick it out just a bit longer, he too can find his way out of the maze.

The young are also highly structured in terms of law. Lots of things adults do are illegal when kids do them—drinking alcohol, and sometimes smoking cigarettes, to say nothing of pot; driving cars under age sixteen or eighteen; and being in certain places, like cocktail lounges or betting establishments or X-rated movies. Anytime anyone looks at our jail problem, it turns out that a third of the inmates in the county or city jail are kids, who are often guilty of no adult crime. And if you want to find out all about the fairness and justice of the police, stick a fright wig on and walk around. The odds are high you'll be stopped in minutes. The odds are also high in too many cities and towns that you'll be the one arrested for doing twenty-seven in a twenty-five-mile-an-hour zone. To the kids, adults are around to kick them into shape or punish them if they misbehave.

A large number of elders, observing what seems to be a frightening lack of discipline among the young, suggest that more discipline is the answer. More rules, more controls, more pressures, until the little creeps shape up, by golly! Maybe if we put the whole generation in jail for a while, they'll be all right. This technique misses the point on two counts—first, the controls already are very tight, and, second, more controls will cost more than anyone is willing to pay. After all, who wants to pay more taxes for more truant officers, more jails, more cops, more surveillance in the schools?

Just being young means that you don't yet know what you like or dislike, and the structured routines of low-level jobs, military service, high school, and college surely don't give one much of a chance to find out. Hence we discover that the young, more than any other

age group, get together in informal groupings of un-
selected people. The young support movies these days
—it's a way to get together with your girl and lots of
other young people. They buy rock-concert tickets, loll
around on the campus green, cluster in malt shops or
something worse, and generally explore their world and
the other young in it. For many a pleasant suburban kid,
locked until eighteen into an immobile world miles from
anything interesting, the real fun part of college, the
Army, or his first job is the chance to move around and
talk to other young people. The young like cities, particularly old-fashioned downtowns—that's where they
can see things happen, smell the excitement, drink in
new ideas. Walk around a downtown of any city—see the
little old ladies, the mature matrons who still occasionally shop there, and most of all, the young. Hippies and
other deviants, who like the city because it's cheap and
anonymous, are there too, with lots of ordinary young
people, wandering around the way we all used to do.

Young people today on the average tend to be much
more aware of their world and what's going on in it. In
spite of all criticism, education is much better than it
used to be, and television helps too—by the time a young
person is eighteen, he has already received more information than the typical pre-1945 adult did in his entire
seventy-year life. This knowledge is what makes the
structure of a youngster's life so painful. One usually
doesn't worry much about unknown options, but to see
them tantalizingly hung out there and be unable to grab
them can be rough. That, *perhaps*, is the story of this
younger generation.

And the young will find that good jobs are going to be
very hard to get all through the 1970s and on to 1984.
This problem leads to the forecast that we will see a lot
of youthful preoccupation with jobs and economics.
Plenty of people want in, one way or another, and the
only way we know how to get them in is through some

kind of economic growth. We may, particularly if liberals obtain power, see huge expansions of the more meaningless kinds of government programs with no visible output, such as educational upgrading (without mentioning norms), relieving poverty (without measuring what's happening), all combined in a sort of big Bureau of Indian Affairs, where lots of sharp young people vie with each other within the system for whatever seems important to them. It's all sort of gloomy, but, it is a realistic projection for the 1970s and early 1980s, which gets back to the peculiar demographic pattern we now have.

Most young people are poor, a dubious proposition to the older, more affluent types, who see in such proposals higher taxes, lower incomes, and less power. The 1972 election suggested that this kind of confrontation between the young articulate have-nots and the older haves is likely to continue, without resolution, for a long time to come.

In fairness to the young, they tend to be much more idealistic than the old folks. A surprisingly large number of them really are idealistic—perhaps the lockstep world they are accustomed to makes them much more sensitive to the plight of their fellow men. The young have historically been the reformers, and they probably always will be. On occasion, they can really shame their elders about injustices, and a good thing, too. Older, maybe wiser heads can argue about the practicality of some of the wilder proposals to correct perceived injustices, but no one can deny the real emotion and deep feelings the young have for those much worse off than they. We are likely to lose much of this in the early 1980s, as the percentage of younger people in our society declines. It will be a quieter world, and maybe a less caring one. The older persons owe much to the young on this point, although few would admit it.

The young tend to respond rather predictably to their

problems in other ways. One thing they are doing is lowering the birthrate sharply. Already in 1973, we are within a hairsbreadth of being at zero population-growth. Given today's much larger number of women at childbearing age, this trend has confounded demographers and forecasters. But since it's happening, one result is that eighteen to twenty-two years from now a much different population will be older, possibly more conservative, and maybe even wiser. Indeed, right now, in these United States the mean age of our population grows steadily older, because the number of births has been dropping for the past twelve years. The big problems of the young now will be very different in 1984 because there are more young now than there will be then.

If present trends continue much longer, the United States may well become a country of negative population-growth. At that point, we may be campaigning to get more children. Or we might start rethinking our immigration laws. If our own young won't have children, maybe we should import somebody who wants to enjoy the benefits of the American economy. We are likely to be in for some real surprises along these lines in the next eleven years. Hang on—most of the persons most concerned with problems of the young and population haven't bothered to think through what our present demographic pattern will lead to.

It might lead to a new puritanism. Already, something is in the wind. Casual listening to the songs the young sing suggest that the discordancies of the late 1960s are gone, replaced by something which sounds vaguely like the 1930s. The churches which have the strictest creeds and are the most dogmatic are growing fast, while more liberal churches decline. And not all the new members are old, by a long shot. In classrooms, the air is now very sober, not at all like the wild times a few years back. Not too long ago, riots and rebellions were the name of the game, mainly on university campuses, and mainly directed at the Vietnam war, the draft, and on occasion, poverty and social injustices. Now the campus (like every place) is relatively quiet. The heat is on, the young know it, and they are responding rather predictably.

If the new puritanism comes in strong, there won't be many riots. The young firebrand blacks, newly arrived on campus, are too busy studying to mess with such nonsense. They have learned, like lots of class-jumping blue-collar background young whites before them, that to win you have to qualify. Have you seen a college-level text in chemistry or math recently? It spells work, man, work! The young whites are nervous about their jobs after getting out, so they would just as soon work too. And besides, somewhat older ex-students learned a few years back that after the hassling dies down, nothing much changes anyhow. Now, if you can get to be a medical doctor and *then* start doing something with the AMA, well, it's worth the effort. And if you can't make it to med school, at least you may be able to find some good job if you behave.

Now combine this attitude with tough economic sledding, and it is easy to forecast that the next eleven years will see a lot of wandering young minstrels roving around the Republic, sometimes raising hell, but more often than not just being apathetic. Except for their concerned families, no one will much care. Like bums in other generations, they will be pushed around by the police and local vigilante committees. The most likely spots for them to light will be on some abandoned farm or another, trying to make a go of it communally or individually, or in the inner city, where lots of abandoned houses now exist, and more are to come. This won't save the city, but it seems like a logical place for a guy with no place to go to end up.

A related life style, which seems to be getting very feasible, is to retire when one finishes college, at age eighteen, or maybe twenty-one. One unanticipated result of very high wages for low-level work is that a person willing to do just a little for society can loaf around most of the time. When you can make a hundred dollars per week for a few weeks working at some assembly line job, you can move in with four to ten others and get your rent and utility bill down to under fifty dollars a month. Add in food costs, plus some used clothes from the Salvation Army or the nearest charity store or rummage sale, and you can live happily for a hundred a month. If you get sick (which is unlikely, at this age), you can go to the free clinic for a shot. Unlike the old, the retired young don't have too many health problems.

One of them explained it all to me. "Look, you'll work for forty years, busting your gut, and maybe getting a heart attack before you retire at sixty-five. And after you've done all that, you can retire and live like I am right now. Why go through those forty years?"

Incidentally, observation of the style suggests that TV and hi-fi sets are in the picture. Often there is a phone, too, and typically wheels, either a couple of motorcycles or an old Chevvy van. And curiously, these groups often seem very interested in learning craft skills. Books on how to fix electric wiring, how to keep your old Volkswagen alive, and similar things are bestsellers in this crowd. If you have endless time, a beat-up old TV set, and a 1961 car, you may as well fix the things and get the satisfaction of doing something useful. Moreover, if you succeed, your need for cash goes way down, and you have yet more leisure time.

The life style of the youthful retiree is missing just one component—satisfaction of the need to achieve something, whatever it may be. It also may well preclude the social approval so many of us, including the young, need so badly. One notes that after a year or so, this type of retirement often ends. With a sigh, the young person returns to the system, often considerably wiser than he was when he left it. We are still a work-oriented culture, and it is still necessary for most of us to do something useful with our lives, however humble it may be.

Only rich countries can afford to allow young people to live their own way, and only in this generation have enough people been rich enough so that this sort of thing can happen. Rich cultures can be tolerant cultures, and America is now the richest. In countries where poverty is common, only a few playboys can do what hundreds of thousands of young Americans take for granted. And the older people who are most critical of the various youth subcultures are those who are not very affluent— they had to work hard all their lives, and it often gripes them to see young people tossing away what they would have given almost anything to have.

So in the end, how different are the young? Until they get their driver's license and access to a car, very different. But when they finally get their wheels, they travel more than the rest of us. They don't have the higher economic base to work from, so they can't afford all the options that their more affluent elders can. They tend to cluster together in less well-defined and more volatile groups, since they are still finding out a lot about themselves and the world. And the more affluent ones try all sorts of odd life styles because they too, particularly during the period immediately after college, have time and a bit of money to try anything once. Some drop out and join the underground, whatever that is. Some of them rebel briefly against the rigidities and structure they find themselves in, and come back. Most of the young, however, are working pretty hard to get to be just like their elders. The good job, the good education, the good income—plus all the freedom instruments—are not a bad deal for anyone, including the young. So they sweat the structure, endure the rigidities, and finally get out the other end with a halfway decent job about like everyone else.

## The Old

It's hard to remember that only thirty years ago, since few old people had pensions or money, they had only a few dismal options. They could go to the poor farm and rot; they could live with their younger relatives; or they could eke out a precarious existence on some marginal farm, trying to get by as long as their health held out. Once you passed sixty-five, you had had it. Our standard ethic was to push all the problems of the old on to their relatives. Only since 1937 have we had a social security scheme with pensions for most workers, and only in the past few years (and maybe not even now) have the aged, or even a significant fraction of them, had enough income to enjoy even modest options. By 1984 it seems clear that these options may grow even more. The old, like the rest of us, have begun to find new choices and freedoms among their traditional problems.

The real bomb, although no one seemed to notice it at the time, was the advent of social security. For the first time in American history, every workingman and his wife were given an earned right to their pension. Until 1937, if you stopped working, you usually stopped earning, unless you were one of the fortunate few who either had a wealthy child to send along a check, or who could have saved enough to buy a private annuity. Ninety-five per cent or more of the old could do neither. Their options were harsh and simple.

Along with social security came a few special deals, affecting hundreds of thousands of workers, such as railroad pensions, state government pensions, teacher-pension systems, and shortly thereafter, company pensions as a part of the union-management bargaining packages. By 1950, many retirees discovered that they had enough money to chose a life style—and increasingly, they did. Instead of the son or daughter telling them what to do (politely, but irrevocably, nonetheless), or worse, having some local welfare official doing the telling, the old folks began to do what *they* wanted. It was their money and their life, so they did what they felt was best.

What was best for them turned out to be lots of different things. *Best* involves, not unnaturally, lots of electric appliances, to ease the labor for older and aching muscles. Even simpleminded peasant women, over from the old country in 1914 with a third-grade education, and used to working very hard around the house, found out about vacuum cleaners, garbage disposals, and automatic washers. Husbands found out about quarter-inch electric drills, garden tractors, and electric lawn mowers. Often these electric helpers were bought in the high-income period just before retirement, when the kids were gone and when a man's income reached new highs, because both of seniority and general prosperity. *Best* involves television, to a degree not often appreciated. TV means free entertainment, the whole world at the flick of a switch, access to what's going on, all without leaving home. Of course, retirees have all the time in the world to watch. *Best* means telephones, so the grandchildren and the doctor are only seconds away, along with the repairmen, the grocer, and anyone else worth talking to when one is old and finds moving about a chore.

But best above all means selective privacy. Instead of relying on children for support, living with *their* friends, eating *their* food, best really means being alone and liking it. Until very recently, the extended American family was common. Grandma or Grandpa or Aunt Sophie were always around in a corner someplace, because there was no other place for them to go. Starting with affluence and pensions, the old folks got out and stayed out as fast as they could. Whatever they wanted to do, they wanted to do it alone.

The usual allegation is that the heartless young, selfishly concerned with their own interests and life styles, don't want the old folks around. More often than not, the truth is just the reverse—the old folks don't want to be watched, criticized, or annoyed by those silly young people. Better to get to Florida, get to the country home, get anyplace, and let the younger relatives come visit them.

This trend, which really began in the 1950s, keeps on accelerating. Now, about half of our nineteen million citizens over sixty-five are still so poor that they have very few options. But social security payments keep rising, and so do other pension-plan payments. Each year, a few more of the old get enough money to do their thing, or at least to widen their options. And they proceed to do it their way, no matter what anyone else thinks. When you're seventy, the fact that some people raise their eyebrows about your behavior doesn't mean all that much. By 1984 a great many of the old will be doing what they want, simply because they will be able to afford to. And what they want, like the life styles of the young, is likely to be all sorts of things.

Older people do worry particularly about two key problems. One is illness and health. With American life expectancies for women in the early seventies, and for men in the late sixties, older people need lots of medical care, and they know it. Medicare has taken some of the economic sting out of being old, but there has been surprisingly little effective medical research into geriatrics. Hopefully there will be more in the future, since the nicest present this world could give its older citizens would be a way of prolonging a healthy, mentally alert life. Too many older people are now living animals, because no one knows what to do for their many and varied maladies. And too many, in spite of Medicare, still don't get the kinds of good health care which is available. Both these problems are likely to change for the better.

The second major problem for older people is transportation. It is hard to drive when one's reflexes are slow, and when various minor maladies make one insecure on the road. So, sooner or later, the old give up their cars. Too often they become prisoners of whatever is left of public transit in the areas in which they live. In retirement villages and a few other places, they can use electric golf carts or tricycles, but in many places no really good transportation system does exist, and the old suffer. The kinds of mass transportation being talked about and sometimes even being built in American cities are ill suited for the old, since such systems run from the suburbs to downtown—places typically of little interest to old people. One really nice present for them would be some sort of reasonably priced personal transport system, such as a car which would pick up the little old ladies to take them to town to the shops, to the doctors, to their relatives, and bring them back again.

The old know all about economic insecurity in a way no one under forty-five can ever grasp. This generation was in its thirties when the great depression hit in 1929, and for the following eleven years, the unemployment rate rarely *fell* to under 10 percent. Most of the decade it was over 15 percent, and in a few grim years it reached 40 percent. There was no unemployment insurance, and precious little welfare either. Oldsters remember full well the years of scrounging for a job, any job, the pink slips, the pay cuts, the trying to figure out how to pay the rent next month, and all the rest. They remember how their own kids couldn't go to college because no one had the money, how they worked at some job which was way below their skills, because that was all they could do. They remember their own parents sitting in the corner, waiting to die. They remember World War II as well. They remember the overtime, the big money in defense plants, the tremendous release the war was to a thirty-five-year-old, who for ten years could not get a job, and now found himself loved and wanted and working over-time. They remember the single-minded march toward victory of that war, and they shake their heads about Vietnam, where simply winning was beyond the rules of the game. And when some young fellow or girl to whom history is irrelevant comes along, well, it's hard to tell the young folks just what it was really all about. Better to go off some place, maybe with a bunch of understanding older folks, and swap yarns.

Older women are different too. All through their working lives, the number of women participating in the work force was climbing, but for all their formative years, a woman's place was in the home. Immigrant girls worked as maids or in the needle-trades sweatshops, and maiden ladies from the middle and upper middle classes sometimes were schoolteachers or nurses. Most women stayed home. They had to. Women over sixty remember doing the dishes, laundry, and ironing by hand, to say nothing of pea podding, potato peeling, and chicken plucking. They remember a time when no one except the very rich had refrigerators, so everyone had to get to the store five times as often as they now do, because butter melted and milk soured if you bought too much at one time. Now all the young women seem to be working. Of course they have the electric slaves and the ironless shirts and the cars to run around in. It all seems so new and so different.

Put it all together, and you discover that the old are

indeed different. They will be different in 1984, too. The present fifty-four-year-old is a bit more educated than the current sixty-five-year-old, but not all that much. He probably will have a fatter pension, so he will be able to afford a few more options. And with a bit of medical luck, he may be somewhat healthier for somewhat longer.

What will the oldsters of 1984 do? They will behave just about like everyone else, and they may even enjoy it more. A growing number choosing to live that peculiar style, will take to selective retirement towns, oriented to whatever the old happen to like to do. Normally, this choice involves moving south, where the weather is warm—Florida, Southern California, and Arizona already have received hoards of older citizens looking for the sun and they will get more. Given more money, more awareness of what's going on, and the urge to do what is useful and interesting, lots of older people will pull up stakes and go. Air conditioning, that boon to civilization, plays a big role here, particularly in really warm places. Once again, the electric slaves provide more options.

Some will choose to stay just where they are, with their remaining friends, their memories, and their habits. And others will find compatible smaller towns or smaller houses or apartments in the same town, and remain. Some will take up politics, usually on the local level; some won't even bother to vote. Some will take the grand tour of Europe or the Far East, and some, following earlier habits, will never leave town. Some will develop new and interesting hobbies and even businesses, while others will slump in front of the TV set. Some will enjoy the grandchildren, and others won't speak to their sons-in-law. Some will spend their savings happily, buying things they never felt they could afford, while many, remembering the grim years, will be saving for their old age at ninety-three. Virtually all of them will have plenty of electric gadgets to ease the work, a car as long as they can get a license, a TV set (or two or three), and a telephone. In short, they will exercise their free choices about the way they please, whether the rest of us like it or not. One thing they are not likely to do is to stick around with the children. Very, very few older people, given a choice, really want to stick with the kids.

For fairly irrational reasons, we as a society have decided that at sixty-five, you've had it. Out and on to retirement, out of the world where things happen and where work is to be done and money made, out to a world of the old. (It's no accident that people who own or control the job as small businessmen and key executives, keep right on working until they drop—this is a fun world for a guy or girl now old and gray.) And just as you get tossed aside, the probability of losing your wife, or even more commonly, your husband in death rises astronomically. And we find the very old, living alone, trying to cope with a major set of adjustments to their historic life styles, getting weak, susceptible to the diseases of old age, becoming unable to perform routinely the tasks accepted as necessary in our society, like cleaning the kitchen or driving to the store. It's a wonder that the old people can adjust and have as much fun as they do. But they were a tough bunch to begin with. Anyone who has had to begin close to the real world of 1884 (and the real world of 1903, particularly on the farm, was not much different), to live through the first mass introduction of all the tools, gadgets, and thinking that began the real world of 1984, to survive two world wars and a couple of nasty panics and depressions, to work hard all his life and still maintain even a semblance of sanity has got to be tough. The old fellows you see walking slowly down to the store or the little widow sitting on the park bench in Florida or the old gaffer pottering in his little garden have all seen and adjusted to a lot. They can and will live a life style which bothers us, but which, given the money and the options, makes a lot of sense to them. They will be tough in 1984 too, and they will have worked out, with a bit of luck, even more diverse life styles than they now have. And the peculiar part of it all is that they may even have lots of fun doing it.

## The Losers

The top 90 percent or so of all American families can enjoy, or try to, the kinds of 1984 we have been talking about. But the bottom tenth or so cannot—they are the losers. They are the families whose incomes are so low as to preclude buying the consumer goods—the cars, electronic gadgets, and such—which enable one to enjoy the new life. A key characteristic of the new life is the income necessary to provide basic necessities, such as decent food, clothing, and shelter, and then have something left over to have fun on. And without that income, not much new living gets done. Of course, poverty is socioeconomic, not just economic. You can readily see how we intuitively put in the socio part when you consider that one of the largest blocks of poor people in the United States today is college students. Yet few would argue that they need much help. Indeed, when a student gets food stamps or welfare money, the public is shocked —such persons don't *deserve* assistance. The reason is that their poverty is very temporary, and, upon gradua- tion, they move rather quickly into the affluent life. What support they get tends to be in the form of scholarships or loans designed to allow them to complete their educa- tions.

The rediscovery of poverty in the early 1960s, and the resultant antipoverty programs have led to much knowl- edge about who is poor. It is a depressing picture. The typical poor family is headed by a badly educated person (often female), perhaps from a minority group, who may well be over sixty-five; and who lacks the basic industrial skills needed to earn enough money to get at the good life. Many of the poor are children, who are members of poor families, and while more black families than white by percentage are poor, more whites (17.4 million) than blacks (8.0 million in 1968) are poor.

One development which could really hurt the present poor is the strict enforcement of efficient antipollution laws. Dirty work is often done by the poor, and rapid economic growth, with many new industrial jobs being created, helps out the unskilled as much as, if not more than, the skilled. If the older plants are closed because they pollute, and if new ones cannot be built, the guy who really suffers is the fellow at the bottom. The highly trained managers and engineers can move across the country to a new job; the poor laborers may not even be able to move across town to find another job, and there may not be one anyhow. They have no options.

One major characteristic of poverty is this lack of options. A poor man does not have the mobility that the affluent do; he does not have the ability to find out about the job market for unskilled laborers in twenty cities; he does not know how to learn new tricks as well as the affluent, because his whole educational background is so limited. Moreover, the affluent (and this includes any family above the ten-thousand-dollar line, or roughly the top half) are pretty good at getting and hanging on to their share. If the ecological shoe is going to pinch, let it pinch someone else.

So, where will we be in 1984? Absolute poverty is likely to be considerably less, which means that the 1984 poor will have a few more options to consider. They will have more income, probably more education and access to information, and a chance to do what others have done, if they so chose. But there will still be a bottom 10 percent, and such persons will still be the losers. It is quite likely that we still will be very worried about such persons in a broader social sense, and the country won't lack for programs and concern in solving the poverty problem.

Romantic talk to the contrary, there is very little evidence that the recently poor behave any differently from the other middle-class types around, and this fact seems to be independent of race. Black families who have finally made it to the lower middle classes are just as interested in getting single family housing, good schools, and all the rest as anybody else.

What poor will be left in 1984? The presently youngish, then middle-aged minorities, particularly black and chicano men, who did not get into the game when young, and who do not have any skills; the deviants of all types, such as young people trying new life styles, far-out radicals who deal themselves out of the game; many sick, such as alcoholics; and perhaps various sexual deviants of the more radical type—whatever *that* may be in 1984. These people will inherit what's left of the inner city, which seems to be the place that no one else wants to be. And of course students will still be poor, though no one is likely to care much.

Another kind of loser, who gets talked about a lot, is the psychological loser. He is a person who, for whatever reason, cannot relate well to the rest of the world. He drinks, has interpersonal problems, finds it impossible to obtain a satisfying job, and has all kinds of personal troubles. In short, he or she is a very unhappy person. Such people come in all income levels, and they are the basis for most of our novels, films, and TV programs. Many tend to be articulate, intelligent, well-educated people, although, contrary to folklore, the majority of such persons are economic losers too. More poor than rich (in proportion to their numbers) have psychological problems, unhappy marriages, and bad job experiences. But the vision of a wealthy man who has everything, but is unhappy, permeates our folklore. It's fun to think that those guys with all the cash are in worse shape than they appear.

Such losers are tragic people, but if they also happen to be middle or upper middle class and affluent, all is not lost. One gets a divorce, but the second marriage may be fine; the rat-race job sometimes is given up, to be replaced by something more meaningful; and psychologists do interesting remedial work with lots of people, to say nothing of such highly personal and successful organizations as Alcoholics Anonymous. Maybe most of us are losers from time to time in this emotional sense, but few are losers all the time. Highly visible they are—but perhaps very numerous they are not.

Any discussion of losers in the United States typically involves only Americans. If others in foreign countries are poor, that is someone else's problem. If Americans are unemployed because South Korean workers are doing a job, the usual reaction is to do something, like impose an import quota, which will screw the Koreans— if they starve, that's their problem! Right now, good Americans are unemployed.

The real losers from now to 1984 will not be Americans, but all the citizens of poor countries who are *really* poor, in a stinking, starvation sort of poverty that few Americans have ever seen, or wish to worry about. The Calcutta Indian who lives on the street, has a money income of maybe fifty dollars per year, and whose kids literally starve, is the loser—not the poor welfare mother in Chicago, desperately trying to survive on two hundred per month. As the world grows smaller, through cheap transportation and instantaneous communication, we may well spend more time worrying about the real foreign losers—not about the relatively poor American winners. If American income were perfectly distributed, so that every American got an equal share, we would all have about forty-two hundred dollars each per year. But if world income were redistributed, so that every citizen in the world got an equal share, we could only look forward to three hundred dollars each per year. The world is a very poor place. Maybe, by 1984, we will have to be more concerned about that than we now are.

# 11

■ ■

# *Public Life: The Return to Privacy*

Our 1984 citizen, surrounded by and eagerly using his freedom instruments, will be living a largely private life. One key characteristic of all freedom instruments is that they push families and individuals toward freer choices, and it seems likely that these will increasingly result in a sort of 1984 medieval manor, with electronic and electrical slaves for assistance, rather than serfs, and with private cars around for transportation rather than horses. But private it is likely to be. Those few who want the excitement and nonselectivity of live contact with others will still be around, in cities. Most people, if they really want to get together with others, will be doing it in selective ways, joining their kinds of clubs, religious groups, or avocational clusterings.

Note also that as more and more people move to a more private world, public life tends to deteriorate. This already is beginning to happen and will continue at an accelerating pace. Public libraries are in deep trouble as circulation declines. Why go down to the library, when anyone can afford to buy his own paperbacks? Bus and rapid transit systems everywhere are falling apart. And this will continue, no matter how much federal money is spent on new systems, because the problem is not better equipment or cleaner stations, but simply that most people prefer the private life in one's own automobile.

Even the police are in trouble, as individuals, seeing problems, turn to burglar alarms, private protection systems, and all the rest. Firemen get released in a few towns here and there—costs have reached the point where some citizens apparently feel it is cheaper to take their chances than to pay for general protection. They might be right, too, if they have modern buildings constructed under modern fire codes. At the federal level, no one seems to trust government anymore, and considerable public apathy is noted. Critics state gleefully that this shows how morally decadent we are, but they miss the key point, namely, that most people are totally unaffected by the vast majority of government programs, so they just don't care. Galbraith pointed out this starvation of the public sector in *The Affluent Society* in 1958 and suggested taxing more from the private sector to spend on the public. For obvious reasons, this idea was widely hailed in government circles, although no one seems to have considered that a majority of citizens prefer the private sector and can do quite well without lots of the public services and goods which they are supposed to be demanding.

The move from public to private was very noticeable in the 1972 presidential election, where nothing was as it used to be. Historic coalitions collapsed, and prognosticators seemed unable to sort out what was really going on. Why did the election campaign go as it did? Increasingly, in the United States, with growing affluence and growing use of the freedom instruments, many people are shifting from the big to the small. That is, instead of relying on big organizations, public or private, for their amusements, life styles, and avocations, they are turning to the home, the family, and the small self-selective organization to get their satisfactions. Even in the job market, a surprisingly large number of people still rely on small units for support. Remember the millions of self-employed professionals, such as doctors, dentists, and lawyers, who work for one- or two-man systems; the millions who still work for smaller companies; the several million small businessmen; and so on down to those who work for county government, which they see as small. Not everyone is employed by General Motors or the Pentagon.

As one shifts to the smaller units, interest in what the big operations are doing tends to fade—it just doesn't matter. And as more people shift this way, public life tends to change dramatically. We all have *some* government programs which are very important to us—educators watch school appropriations; farmers pay close attention to farm legislation; and aerospace firms push for more defense appropriations. But if the impact of your game is seen as distant and irrelevant, and if I, one of 210 million people, cannot really do much influencing, why bother to get involved?

There is a curious dichotomy here. When it is noted that we have big problems, and that they require big organizations to cope with them, one senses that no one is really listening or believing any more. The new organization won't save us, and very likely it won't work at even minimal levels of efficiency. All it will do is cost us taxpayers something. So new big things are having trouble getting started. If the use of freedom instruments is going to increase as expected, then lots of government is in deep trouble, and will continue to be long after 1984.

People aren't dumb, and they don't like to be pushed around. Because the freedom instruments give individuals more choices, power becomes increasingly hard to come by, when everybody is out there doing something they want to do, not what their elected leaders want them to do. And when given a choice between something which gives the individual more choice and something else which gives someone else the power, most people opt for more freedom. We use cars instead of buses; we watch television rather than go to the movies; and we do our washing in our own washers at the time of our own choice, rather than use a laundry. In each case, the choices of when to do it, how to do it, and where to do it are made by the individuals, not the managers or administrators. People like it this way, even if power brokers do not. In any case, the long term result is a steady erosion of public power.

You can test this for yourself by considering just how often you are at the mercy of authority. If you are young and in school, the answer is "lots of times." If you are old and immobile, again you are at the mercy of whatever passes for a public transport system. And if you are poor, you have to put up with the fumblings of welfare agencies, poverty planners, and all the rest. But if you are reasonably affluent, aged twenty-one to sixty-five, own a car, and have the other freedom instruments, it is surprising how difficult it is to control you. Your boss has some control, since he signs the payroll. The traffic cops also have some modest control. And at a faceless distance, such organizations as zoning commissions and tax authorities have something to say about your life. But you have probably escaped, a long time ago, the tyranny of close in neighbors, bus companies, entertainment systems such as movie houses, high-density controls so common in central cities, many service establishments, and much, much more. The reason is that you do it yourself, so to hell with them. And the more you do yourself, such as fixing your own car or washing machine, the less you are controlled by others.

This shift to a private life spells lots of trouble for all governments and many kinds of public activities, all the way down to school board meetings and zoning authorities. We are already seeing many fewer public gatherings, as politicians and planners sense that most people will just stay away. Only when one's personal life is directly threatened, as when the freeway is about to be put through your living room, or your kids' school is being menaced by rapists or drug pushers, will the people show up. In such cases, they can be very vociferous and ingenious in showing their displeasure, which often leads to lively newspaper coverage and the feeling that the public meeting is not dead. But in far too many cities and towns, a routine, yet important zoning or city council meeting which might have significant long-term consequences for many citizens goes virtually unattended.

For the past twenty-five years, the biggest growth sector in the economy has been local government (state, country, and city). We seem to require endless civil servants to handle our increasingly complex problems. But note what is going to happen. Increasingly we see that the more government we have, the less gets done. That is, with some notable exceptions, government hasn't produced. We hire more police, and get more crime. We add more control commissions to protect us, and we get exploited in about the same old way—only this time, with government sanction. One senses that the taxpayers are beginning to see the point—and, given that an increasing number of them are out in the suburbs or country, we may just find out that we don't need all that government concern any more.

If the police, pressured by righteous citizens, keep on

arresting people for victimless crimes, such as smoking pot and being drunk, don't bet too much on police power being very important in 1984. One big advantage of freedom instruments is freedom from public investigation. What I do in my house is my business, and as long as I don't frighten the neighbors, no one will bother me. If I can drive with reasonable safety and within traffic regulations, I won't get bothered in my car either, which is more than you can say for the old life style in some crowded city.

Once again, we see individuals and families making their own quite rational adjustments to a given situation. If crime rises, go away from it, since you cannot do much about it as an individual. If the police report for the thirty-eighth straight year that crime has risen, and then ask for more money to fight it, just yawn and go back to preparing a gourmet dinner. It may be true, and you may even be a victim, but you can easily minimize your risks by taking full advantage of the freedom instruments. In short, live a more private life.

Perceptive law enforcement officials are beginning to see this point—they know that law and order gains real respectability when policemen fight the kinds of crime which do bother citizens, such as assault, rape, murder, armed robbery, and other types of violence against others. Perhaps by 1984, we will have a much more rational attitude toward what we are trying to do with our police forces. Remember also, that mind-bending drugs and other forms of behavioral control against violent deviants will be available (they already are). Moreover, crime-fighting technology continues to advance pretty fast, and various types of electronic gear can be used as efficiently by the police as by anyone else. Add the fact that there will be fewer young people around (and they are the biggest criminally inclined group in the society), and we may find a rather nice world in 1984. Crime will be down, because as people scatter out more, crimes related to density decline. One cannot mug a person unless one can find a victim, and victims are hard to find in a very diffuse population. In cases where criminal acts do occur, it is possible by 1984 that we will know much more about how to handle and cure deviant behavior than we now do.

But governments are not likely to commit suicide by voluntarily going out of business, and it is unlikely that governments or various subsets of city government are going to be abolished either. Curious statistic—since 1930, the percentage of the work force doing government work and the percentage doing servant work have just reversed. All the servants we can't get (and maybe don't want anyhow) have shifted into government offices.

Governments are likely to respond by trying to figure out what citizens do want, and then trying to provide it. This may be very hard to do, since a lot of government at all levels *is* irrelevant. School problems will still be with us, and local government will try to meet whatever needs are expressed in this major sector. Given the trend to continuing education, we may see major experiments in school for all, not just for the young. Already we have many prototypes: night-school classes in high schools and college extensions, open universities, where any serious student of any subject and any age can enroll. If a welder wants to obtain an engineering degree to advance himself, why not? If he is forty and didn't finish high school, who cares? Such pupils often are the smartest and most motivated.

Traffic control will be with us for a long time, as will land-use zoning. No one wants a high-rise apartment or a pig farm next to his nice new suburban house, and such zoning issues get much attention. They will continue to. Traditional local-government activities involving property registration and transfers, cleaning up of public land, and keeping the streets clean will be around for a long time, as will sidewalk repair and construction.

If we get into a major energy crisis, we could have a real political fight. Present government attitudes seem to push us in this direction. Various public utility commissions, for political reasons, seem unwilling to allow necessary price increases for prime sorts of raw energy (e.g., natural gas). They fear that when consumers' bills go up, they will scream. So the price is kept artificially low and consumption is higher than it might otherwise be. Also the ecology movement has effectively prevented construction of many electric power plants and oil and gas pipelines. Sooner or later, probably sooner, there will be some major crisis, like New York City without electric power for perhaps a week. By the time this crisis passes, both the ecologists and other antipower groups are going to feel lots of heat. The freedom instruments, all of them, need energy to work. Without gas, our cars don't run, without electricity, our slaves don't work. And this could really get people mad. The crisis could also lead to accelerated research for a way to beat the game, like self-contained fuel cells for each house. If the so and so's can't even get me my power, some private firm just might be able to. And if we do get very reliable low-cost individual power units, scratch one more public political problem. The Federal Power Commission will undoubtedly still go through its incantations, but no one will notice.

Another major public issue will be jobs and income, particularly for the young. And a lot of older persons will join in their concern (if it's *your* son or daughter who can't get a good job, you worry too). Various minority groups, including women, will still fight for equal pay and rights on the job market, hopefully with much more success than they have had to date. Our expectations about jobs, thanks to all our education, including the informal kind we get from TV and movies, will continue to outrun realities on the job market.

We can also expect lots of static about the usual economic problems, such as inflation and income distribution, particularly if the freedom instruments are affected very much. A curious trend is that for the past twenty years, the prices of most freedom instruments have held steady or declined in real terms. TV sets and other electronic devices are cheaper than they were in 1955, and a lot better and more reliable too; telephone service is not much more expensive, and some of it, like long distance calls, is much cheaper; and even autos have not changed much in price, particularly if you allow for quality changes and used-car availability and prices. White goods, such as washers and refrigerators, also have remained rather steady in price, as incomes have risen.

Our bureaucracies are going to become an issue. The mayors, governors, and presidents come and go, but the bureaucrats remain, operating agencies that were set up with very good intentions to handle the problems of 1935 or 1953. Many are so antiquated that they are probably dysfunctional, yet they go on and on. A good mayor, trying to get something done, finds that he can't fire the sanitation department manager, who doesn't like his new policies—so there is no improvement in garbage collection. In the end, the disgusted citizen votes with his feet and goes someplace else, leaving behind a dreary procession of decaying agencies, each convinced of its own omnipotence, each totally out of touch with what is really going on.

So far, we have been too busy creating new bureaucracies to worry much about the total failures. Yet when we discover that schools cannot educate; police cannot cut crime; firemen cannot stop blazes, armies cannot win wars, garbagemen cannot remove refuse; street repair gangs cannot fix streets; Indian affairs bureaus cannot help Indians; transportation commissions cannot control transport—then why have all of them? At the local level, in far too many cities, any citizen naive enough to think that his local government agencies are working for him quickly learns differently. The police are more interested in retirement benefits than crime prevention, the sewer inspectors like payoffs more than fixing sewers, and so on. Better to go somewhere else and not pay taxes for something you're not getting.

Getting rid of the deadwood has been a popular cry for a long time in politics, but now the total incompetence is getting ridiculous in far too many places. Lots of quite decent, sober Americans have reached the point where they automatically (and too often correctly) perceive *any* government agency as interested only in their exploitation and victimization, even when the agency is supposed to be their protector. Now all of this may be unfair to many hard-working and dedicated government personnel. But given the way freedom instruments start changing things, the public's tendency to feel abused may be inevitable. One sure forecast is that those agencies with enough sense to do some deep thinking about their mission and what they can do to help their clientele, are likely to flourish, while those agencies who think that because they are there they have the right to remain are in for trouble. Would you believe abolishing a whole school system or police department? It just might happen.

Many major national issues which have been critical in the past few decades may well decline in importance by 1984. It already seems pretty clear that foreign affairs as a major concern has had it, and that we are likely to enter, for better or worse, a long period of neo-isolation. For the typical American, sitting in his private castle, foreign affairs aren't too important. And with the decline in interest in foreign affairs will come the end of the draft. Given what else is going on, and how young men regard this problem, it is probably unenforcible anyhow.

Cities and urban problems are likely to fade as issues too, because most people won't be there any more, and hence they won't much care. Just as the farm issue has retreated from a matter of general concern thirty years ago to one affecting a relatively small pressure group, so will the city issues fade. But if too many national tax resources are devoted to cities, people living elsewhere will object, and then there may be a brief flurry of concern.

Poverty and welfare are also likely to be relatively smaller issues. Fewer people are likely to be really poor —rising incomes, plus more generous pensions, will take care of more people. And we may, sooner or later, forget the moral issue and just send money to the poor. If we do this (as President Nixon has already suggested, and as many more politicians will before the 1970s are out), then public concern will diminish. Once we agree to share the wealth in some way, we can forget the problem. If the poor stay sociologically poor, that's their problem. This somewhat more cold-blooded approach to poverty results from our 1970s experience with reform. It hasn't worked well, and really efficient abolition of sociological poverty costs more than most taxpayers are willing to pay.

Ecology may also be slipping as a major issue in the 1970s, particularly if the billions being spent and about to be spent on this problem pay off. By 1984, lots of pollution problems which seemed very tough to solve in 1973, will have been solved. Moreover the freedom instruments all work fine without much pollution, *if* we use some common sense about energy policies and auto use and design. Lots of freedom-instrument use may actually become less polluting. We could have no more newspapers, as one example, since your electronic cable system could give you the news on a screen. If you wanted to save something, a printout could be made of that item alone. Just this one development would do much to save paper. And we are really pressed for energy, and if energy costs go way up (say, for gasoline), we may well use the phone (and TV phones) more and our cars less.

Many politicians have badly misjudged how quickly the freedom instruments are changing, at an accelerating rate, the nature of American politics and public life. The political process used to involve individuals directly, in terms of life style, protection, income, jobs, recreations, and all the rest. But now increasing numbers of citizens do not plan to use their parks, their libraries, their welfare funds, their bus systems, their defense facilities, their research report, or their anything elses. Roads are supported, because people use them; enough people have children in school to care about educational policy and spending. And most people will support some modest level of police and fire protection. So we find a taxpayer's revolt. Why not? As the trend continues toward the private life and fewer children, expect more revolts, not fewer.

As the bulk of Americans are rapidly adopting this hands-off attitude, the various professional pressure groups will fight it out, not the people themselves. More and more of the political process will be transacted by the pros—the lobbyists for the various interests. This trend is well along—you can see it at work any day if you read the newspapers. Farmers want this; railroads want that; a trade union wants something else. Such pressures tend to come from producers, since they are very well organized, and they have a lot to gain. A minute change in sugar import quotas of no importance to the general public can mean tens of millions in profits for the refiners. A new air route awarded between Chicago and New

York is worth $200 or $300 million in cash. For that kind of money, every airline in the country has one of its best brains in Washington, figuring out how to get them (footnote—if the real payouts are in pieces of paper obtained in Washington, the best corporate brains will be there scheming, not operating airlines across the country. Who then takes care of the consumer?).

The various forms of the consumer-protection movement offers a counterreaction to such producer pressures, and enough consumers feel abused that such movements are growing and may continue growing for a decade or more. But their solutions, however, are interesting—they want still more control, more government to save me from myself. I hope they have fun, but I rather like the idea of being able to chose things that are unsafe, immoral, or chintzy. Maybe that's a freedom I would like.

A real problem which we will be talking about a lot in 1984 is just how far the retreat to privacy can go before the whole society starts coming unstuck. A city may go broke, because most people do not care enough to save it—but what then? It will still be there, very troubled, and it will still have lots of people in it. What do we do? No one really knows. Or, if we are all dispersed in our cozy suburban castles, enjoying our freedom, some other country, perhaps more disciplined, may see a great opportunity to take military action. It has happened before in human history, and it may happen again. How do we handle this, if we are living totally private lives? Is sending money to handle the troubles of the poor and aged enough? If the troubled are merely shoved aside, even on good incomes, what then? We just don't know. Some thoughtful people would argue that already we have gone too far, that we should begin to turn back to the ways man used to live. Clearly, most Americans would disagree.

Unfortunately to date, the return to older ways is cloaked in the jargon of a return to the 1930 city. Most Americans, having happily escaped that particular life style, would not be the least bit interested in returning to it. Surely there are other ways that can restore the sense of community. Our imagination fails us—not surprising, since this whole mass-privacy movement is only a few decades old. But in the end, this may be the most critical political question of all, since the very survival of the nation will depend on how we figure it out. In any case, we seem destined to live much more private lives than we have historically.

It should go something like this: A typical 1984 middle American sits, as usual, in his exurban home. It's not exactly a palace, like those big jobs the rich have, way out in the country—indeed, the house was built in 1962. But it has a half-acre lot, lots of electric power, and all the freedom instruments at hand.

Our citizen turns on his TV (wall-screen-size, of course), and watches the news. It seems that Central City just defaulted on its bond issues. The city finally is broke. Grave city officials are interviewed; the reporter talks to firemen whose checks did not arrive; and a police commissioner speculates about what will happen when the police are not at hand.

Who cares? Not this citizen. He doesn't own any of the bonds, nor does he even go to the city anymore. Like most Americans (starting as far back as 1972), he works in an office in the suburbs, out along the freeway, in a nice, tree-shaded park. He doesn't need the central-city police—indeed, his suburb, which has fought for thirty years to stay politically independent, has actually cut its police force by half in the past five years. Their new mayor pointed out that, after all, virtually all homes had some form of private protection, ranging from police dogs to good locks to complex electronic surveillance devices. Crime rates had been falling fast, so why hire more cops? Moreover, the new supreme court rulings that no one could be arrested for a victimless crime, such as public drunkeness, gambling, abortion, or drug taking, meant that about half the crimes of 1980 were now not crimes at all. One result was that the police had a lot less to do. Taxpayers had voted for more government economy, so why not cut the force? Our citizen notes with satisfaction that he had enough sense to get out of the city many years ago, when his kids began to go to school. It was a lot nicer out here, particularly when the company where he had his office job also moved out.

The new suburban mayor had cut the fire department in half, too. This suburb had been built largely after 1960, under quite effective fire codes, and there was little chance of any major conflagration. Housewives still had kitchen fires, and kids still occasionally set small fires while playing with matches, but the new electronic-surveillance system which had been installed in 1980 in every building meant that alarms were automatic and quicker, and fewer men could get to the blaze faster. Moreover, they had much superior fire-fighting chemicals. Was it any wonder the department had its budget cut? The city still had the old-fashioned warehouse and tenement fires that were very tough to control, so they had a huge fire department. But, as one cynic had noted, since most of the fires seemed to be in empty buildings, why not just let them burn down?

The TV reporter turned next to the school problem. Our average man was interested in that, since he had two kids in grade school. Curiously, the bankrupt city would not close the schools—the 1976 law which allowed any parent to chose any school he or she wanted and pay for it through the federal school-voucher program, meant that the schools that had lots of students kept getting their money. Those that could not attract students were in such tough shape that no one cared anyhow.

Our citizen was satisfied with that solution. He liked the idea of the federal government giving him chits worth a year's elementary education for each of his children, and he and his wife had done quite a bit of shopping before picking the public schools they sent their children to. When they gave their vouchers to the school, the school had turned them in to the government to get the cash necessary to finance one child per chit. The schools themselves had fought this one bitterly, since by 1976 the birthrate had dropped so low that there was massive excess capacity in the school system. If kids and their parents could decide which school to go to, then how would the poorer schools manage to survive? The answer—they didn't—proved popular with taxpayers and very unpopular with school administrators and teachers. But our friend knew that the school was really trying to do something with his kids—he remembered when he was a boy, schools ran for teachers—now, if you couldn't get the kids to come, the school got its budget cut. His wife had to take the kids to school, which was five miles away, in their second car each day, but they both felt it was well worth it. Buses were still around, but if you chose a school outside your district, you had to figure out how to get the children there.

Our average man was not very average here, since it turned out that most parents stuck by the local schools. It was strange, though, how nice the school administration and teachers were to parents and kids, now that they knew they could lose both pupils and budgets. Everyone had predicted disaster when the new school choice law was passed in 1976, but it had turned out quite differently. Nowadays kids really learned things!

The television commentator was talking now about the crisis in mass transit. Of course the system had been losing tens of millions of dollars every year. Now, with the city broke, it would probably stop running. Passenger traffic had been falling for ten years, or more—now, only 1 percent of workers used the system every day, as compared to 20 percent a few years back. The steady drift of jobs out of town, plus still more cars, had cut that market drastically. If the transit system didn't run, few people would be inconvenienced. The announcer reported that in recent years, most of the loss of traffic was not to cars, but to the new legal jitney system that had been set up in 1980. Those freewheeling cars that picked up just a few people and took them all over the place for a few cents more than the bus fare (and in some cases, even less), seemed to meet the needs of the few who still didn't have cars better than the buses and trains.

Next the zoo manager was interviewed. They were closing his zoo next week, and the animals were being sold off at cut-rate prices to a few other zoos that still existed. Our citizen thought idly about taking the kids to see the animals—they never had—and he remembered with pleasure the trips he had taken with his father when he was a boy. But the kids right now were watching a documentary on the life of lions in Africa on the third TV set in the playroom. They would learn more about tigers and lions in an hour than they would in fifty trips to any zoo.

The bad news continued. The electric company was in deep trouble with the power commission, but our citizen had put in his fuel cell two years back, so he could care less what the electric company did—he wasn't a customer any more. All he did was buy a recharge from General Electric, for a monthly fee of $19.50—his electric bill had been more than that every month, and once in a while they had power failure. The transportation commission was about to cease operations, but again, it didn't seem to matter—he supposed that somehow the freight rates that got charged had something to do with him, but since he never paid freight bills himself, he didn't much care. He recalled that his brother had faced a huge moving bill last year when he changed jobs and moved four hundred miles, but his brother had easily solved that problem by renting a truck and doing it himself—with the help of a couple of college boys who needed the money. The teamster's union and the transport commission were upset by all of this, but there wasn't very much they could do about it—the bill to ban U-haul trucks had been soundly defeated in the legislature a few years back, thanks to major-consumer-group pressure.

At last, the news of gloom in the city was over, and the commentator commenced with the news from the state capital. For the eighteenth straight time, the citizens had voted down a bond issue for parks, schools, and general state expenses. The governor had announced reluctantly that he was forced to cut state services. He ticked off the unlucky ones. State university and college funds were reduced. Our 1984 citizen wasn't worried—college enrollments had been declining, and besides, the voucher system applied to college as well as elementary school. If his kids wanted to go to college, they could get in anyplace that they chose with their chits. But they probably wouldn't try—he thought of the new private, profit-making trade school which had recently opened nearby, offering courses in all sorts of practical and esoteric subjects. He wasn't quite sure what a fuel-cell analyzer did, but his neighbor had that kind of job, and he made seventeen thousand dollars a year. You could learn the business in two years, for two thousand a year. Why not? If the state university's budget got cut, well, that was someone else's problem.

Our friend liked camping, and he had thought of voting for the state bond issue for that reason. But he owned, with five other people, a nice abandoned farm downstate, some forty acres, which was on a country road and all theirs. Every summer, he went down with his wife and kids and camped there for a few weeks. They had a stream (admittedly, that new antipollution law had sure cleaned that up), and he could hunt and fish and relax *his* way, without worrying about game wardens, rangers, or other public officials trying to tell him what to do.

The next news item was upbeat, for a change. The new sewer landfill system was working well. Several suburbs were now dumping their treated sewage on an old strip mine some forty miles away, and the whole area was being reclaimed. Now someone could plant corn there and get good yields, which was nice, because farm exports were still going up, even after all these years. Foreigners, it seemed, were having troubles with too many people and too little agricultural productivity.

Our citizen remembered voting for that bond issue, which had easily passed in the suburban communities which had proposed it. Modern suburbs now had their own home self-contained sewer-disposal system, but older houses like his still needed sewer systems, and the old one had been a mess, always overflowing and smelling. Actually, the taxpayers were winning on this one, since revenues from sales of reclaimed land were more than the bond values.

Our friend was up on this one. He had no garbage service, but rather owned a gadget which chewed up everything and dumped it in the new sewer. The treatment plant was designed to sort out little bits of metal from all the other junk and recycle it, while it further separated paper, glass, and other hard bits from the general guck and recycled them too. What was left was dirty water, human excrement, and other vegetable matter, which got purified and poured in a goosy mess onto that old strip mine. It made a swell topsoil, since it was natural fertilizer. Our 1984 middle American recalled, not all that fondly, when he had to take out the garbage and fight with the collectors about the way his cans were sealed. Now those garbagemen were gone, and this system was a lot nicer.

Our friend thought of the old days, when he had lived in a flat in the city. He had hassled with rent-control specialists, building inspectors, sanitation guys who always seemed to think the building was full of bugs (it was, actually, but the residents didn't much appreciate being reminded of that), the cops who used to come when his neighbor beat up his wife, and a whole group of petty functionaries whose duties were to make life tolerable in the crowded city. Now, out here in the exurb, he still struggled with a few of them. The auto license bureau was a chore, but he managed that. When the new sewers system went in, he had argued with those people too, but that was over when the system was finished. No, life was now a lot simpler, since this way of living involved a lot less messing around with government people.

Our friend turned off the TV, punched his newspaper printout button to get the latest newspaper (printed right in the house, of course, with disappearing ink, so the same paper could be used over, just like an old towel in a public lavatory), and sat down to read. He thought that he should call his mother on the TV telephone that night—hadn't talked to her in a long time, and the kids always enjoyed seeing her. There was a note in the paper that the U.S. Post Office was in deep trouble—people didn't seem to write as many letters as they used to.

Our citizen wondered what he would do this evening —there was always so much to do, and so little time to do it in! He finally went to his TV console, looked up a code number, and dialed the program for those interested in chess. He was a pretty good player—he had come in fifth in the area championships last year—and this new program was supposed to show how a real master handled the Ruy Lopez. The tape came on almost immediately, and he was soon involved in the excitement of the game and the analysis of the moves. All in all, it wasn't a bad way to live.

# 12

■ ■

# Futurology:
# The Real World of 2084

The real world of 1984 we have been talking about is actually quite old: automobiles were around in 1890; the first airplane struggled aloft in 1903; radio waves were known about in 1899; most major household appliances date from the 1920s; even television was first demonstrated in 1929; and electric power and telephones date back at least to the 1880s. What has been happening over the years is that things which are fairly old have been perfected, improved, been reduced in price, and gradually spread to most Americans. The process of change for a long time has been mainly horizontal, not vertical. That is, more and more people get the same things. A rich man had a telephone in 1900; now most people do. Only affluent homes could afford most household appliances in 1925; now they are pervasive.

But once some gadget becomes an item of very common use, it does change the world. Ten thousand telephones or television sets did not make much difference in the way most people lived, but fifty million or more of them did. At some critical point, when distribution gets wide enough, the world is different forevermore. Such things alter life for lots of people—for example, they live longer if everyone gets a polio shot, gets to a hospital, or even finds out about nutrition. There is no question but that the usual gradual innovation and change will continue to occur, and much of it will be in freedom instruments. Cars will undoubtedly be less polluting. Electronics devices will most probably be improved and miniaturized. One can predict safely that television screens will be larger; that appliances will be more efficient and maintenance free; and so on. This type of improvement is not likely to change the world radically, except perhaps to make it a somewhat more pleasant place to be in, with less fuss and bother. But from time to time, we have throughout history had sudden discontinuities in development and such change could, and probably will, happen again.

Three major possibilities might shove us backward. The most obvious example involves pollution. Suppose the crisis biologists are right, and suppose within a few years our atmosphere starts to collapse, or the supply of food is menaced by air pollution, or there is some similar disaster. We would be forced to abandon very quickly most of the freedom instruments we have and go back to our 1930 life style. If it really does turn out that the rapidly growing energy-use system we have been building for so long is ecologically unviable, then we will have to do something drastic, including using less energy on a massive scale. Cars would go for sure, but perhaps, in this world, electronics would stay. Then we would see a lot of communication substituted for transportation. Electronics are appealing in such a world, because not only do they use little materials (which take little energy to make), but also they use very little energy to operate in their modern form.

Another very negative possibility is some form of total war, which wipes out some significant fraction of the human race. If you don't like atomic warfare, consider bacteriological war, laser death-rays, or possibly some form of gas warfare. Few question the fact that such catastrophes are possible, given the present state of scientific knowledge. We have lived in the shadow of the Bomb for twenty-seven years now, and so far, so good. But there is no guarantee that we will be around tomorrow. God only knows what might emerge after the catastrophe.

A final highly negative possibility would be some form of mass mind control. If people won't stay in line, why not manipulate their minds so they will? Scientists seem to be close to developing the necessary drugs, and some half-mad dictator could possibly use them on the whole population.

These three terrible possibilities have one major theme in common—they rather dramatically restrict human choice. And since we have been defining freedom as choice expansion, it is clear why these cataclysmic developments would be so negative. But there are lots of innovative breakthroughs which might provide much more freedom and many more options.

Marge and John Allison are interested in having a child. So they go to the breeder hospital, where Mr. Allison deposits some sperm in a test tube, and Mrs. Allison has a minor operation to obtain an ova. The two good-naturedly discuss what kind of child they want— girl or boy, really smart or just kind of smart (who wants a real genius around the house for twenty years?), blond or brunette, a real athlete or just well built, and so on. Then they place their order. The sperm and ova are joined, some minor adjustments are made, and in nine months the baby is delivered. Mrs. Allison could have carried the baby herself if she chose, but she's working, and it is easier to use the artificial womb. Of course, the baby is a blue-eyed blonde girl, just like they wanted.

Since no one wants to do the dirty, monotonous assembly-line work any more, we decide not to. So we take some chimpanzees, or if we really want some strength, some great apes, do a bit of genetic engineering here and there, and we create some animals which are bred to the assembly line. They work their eight hours a day, and don't mind the boredom a bit—their IQs are barely high enough to get the bolt on the nut, to make the single welding pass, or to put the iron piece in the punch press. Because they have to think hard to figure out what to do, they are not bored at all. And of course we breed into them love, discipline, and affection for men. They don't join unions or strike for more pay, and it costs just two dollars a day to feed and house them.

Booker T. Smith, black, unemployed, semiliterate, born in Mississippi, now a resident of Chicago, contemplates his last futile effort to get a job, and sighs. Who wants an unskilled black man from the Chicago ghetto? So as his last gasp, Mr. Smith signs up for a weird deal he's heard about—something about changing your personality and your color. A few weeks later, Booker T. Smith walks into the employment office and applies for a job. The clerk glances at the tall, handsome, well-built blond, Swedish American. He'd make a good plant guard, in spite of his poor education. The clerk asks, out of curiosity, why the name Booker T.—which he usually associates with blacks. Mr. Smith smiles, ruddy-faced, pushes back his straight blond hair, and says something about how his parents admired the great educator. It really doesn't matter to the clerk, since all he has to do is look at the fellow, and he knows he's trustworthy. The job is his. What Booker T. now realizes is that black is just a couple of chromosomes in your genetic structure. All you have to know is which ones and how to change them just a little bit.

These sorts of genetic engineering are coming, into a world which is decidedly not ready for them. Stating the problem this way seems weird to most people, but recent work in biochemistry and genetics suggests that some forms of genetic engineering may be here sooner than we think—maybe like now, if some lab reports are correct. So far, this engineering involves flatworms or some lower forms of life, but wait a decade or so. Already scientists are deciphering the genetic code, and sooner or later they will be able to change irrevocably the way we live, probably before most of us die. This one could be a high plus for freedom, since it provides a whole string of options which we haven't had before. Like many other developments, it is quite likely that relatively few people would take the options, but the fact they are there is enough. If every black *could* be white, then we would have to figure out some new prejudices, because if we discriminated too much, people would simply change. (Research note: I have discussed this with blacks for about six years now, and increasingly they say that they would stay as they are—black pride is growing. But the very fact that one could change would be enough to blow our present discriminatory pattern—or any other one we could think of which involved what people look like, their sex, or how smart they are.)

Jack Baxter, typical American of 2084, glanced at his stopwatch. He was slowing down—he could only run the kilometer in four minutes flat now, and when he was 80, he could do it in three-fifty. But, being 140 years old made a difference, in spite of what his doctor said. Jack had received his first cancer shot in 1981; he had obtained his mechanical heart in 2014, before they really got those organic ones perfected, so he wasn't a very good specimen of a complete human. But he felt pretty good—he had been one of the lucky ones, who had received his rejuvenation shots before he turned 40, so he was still a young-looking fellow. Of course he looked old in his world, since no one got much beyond 30-looking anymore. And of course he would die—right now, guys pushing 200 were in tough shape and kicking off.

We keep eliminating diseases, so far mainly children's diseases, so most of our modern medicine really is a gift to the young. Most of the decline in mortality has been in the years before twenty, so one huge freedom young people now have is the right to stay alive. But coming down the pike rapidly is the ability to preserve youth (again, a problem, and a complex one, in biochemistry, but solvable, sooner or later); the ability to correct all kinds of cardiovascular problems with new hearts of some sort, and the ability to wipe out cancer. What else is there? We could live a long, long time with this kind of assistance, and the right to stay alive is the biggest freedom of all. Avoid accidents, and drive carefully—you just may be one of the first generation to live a lot longer than the traditional threescore and ten, and you may enjoy whatever happens way on to the twenty-second century if you behave yourself.

Death used to be a pretty simple thing. Body processes stopped, and you left us. But nowadays even, it is not uncommon for a person to be revived with heart massage perhaps a full hour or more after he's "dead." By 2084, if we can get a "corpse" into cold storage soon enough, lots of people who now would die may not. Suspension would very significantly expand our options. Now we all die, sooner or later—maybe by 2084, we won't die until we are damn well good and ready. And that would be a new freedom indeed.

Johnny, who's almost ten, can't read, but no one is worried. Indeed, Johnny has been to school since he was three, but it hasn't been the kind of school that we are familiar with. The kids learn all sorts of things about living together and socializing, but nothing about academic subjects. You see, we have figured out that age ten is about the time that a child can really put reading and mathematical skills to use. So, on his tenth birthday, Johnny goes to the brain-control center. He sits for an hour or so under a gadget that looks something like a hair-dryer, with him plugged into it. When he unplugs, the entire reading, writing, and math patterns he needs to know are impressed directly on his brain. Why mess around for years drilling kids, when all education really consists of is a set of very complex brain patterns? Just instill them directly, and you save lots of time and money. Out in the poor countries, this idea is particularly attractive, because in the old days, people were too poor to have schools. Lots of children never did learn basic skills. But now they do, in an hour, and whole countries can eliminate illiteracy in a few months. And if you want to teach any other kind of skills, like electrical theory for craftsmen, well, there's a pattern for that too. Don't ask me what millions of schoolteachers are going to do—I just see what's coming.

Max Peerson is commuting to work, new style. He's got a 2084 model antigravity space sled, so he goes out to his garage and turns it on. His house is in a peculiar place, by 1973 standards—it's up on top of a mountain, about forty miles from his suburban job, and there are no roads leading to it. There is only one coaxial cable, which ties in his TV-electronic system to the world. The house has a fuel cell for power, and a special waterless garbage-sewage-treatment system which does not need pipes. The big antigravity truck brings in water once a month for other use.

Max turns on his sled and leaves, moving at about fifty feet off the ground, following the old, beat-up freeway, which is now abandoned. He's following level one, north, which keeps him out of the way of people going in other directions, and the minicomputer on his instrument panel keeps him in line. If he gets too close to some one, the automatic repeller would simply slide him up, down, or sideways, so accidents do not happen.

Max gets to work and parks on the roof. There are few parking lots anymore—you can stick a gravity sled almost anyplace, since it can land like a helicopter, straight down. And if Max really wants to see the world, he can pay an extra five thousand dollars, and buy a high altitude (like, up to five thousand miles) sled and really get above it all.

Max is a design engineer for the Acme Boatworks, which used to make atomic submarines. It still does, except that now those submarines (which have been around since the 1950s) are being used as spaceships. Why not? They are completely self-contained, regenerating air, recycling garbage and sewage, and quite capable of staying under water or out in airless space for years. Acme is now booming, since with antigravity the major problem of space travel is now elminated. Getting out of the gravity sink called earth used to take enormous amounts of energy—now, you turn on the antigravity neutralizer, and you go with a ten-thousand-ton ship, with maybe the power needed to run down a modern auto battery. And once you get out in space, you hoist a five-square-mile aluminum-foil sail (remember, in space, there is no gravity—so a thin sail, if extended, stays extended), and use the sun's energy to push you along at steadily increasing velocities. The nearest star is four light years away, and this means that it will take something over four (maybe twenty) years to get there, but why not? There are planets out there to explore and settle. . . .

So Max sits in his office, redesigning his spaceship,

wondering if he, or maybe his kids, should leave the whole damn planet. It really *is* spaceship earth, and so far we're all stuck on it together, but just maybe we'll figure out a cheap way to get off the old world. And if we do, all the doom and gloom about ecological crises and population pressures, and all the rest, gets kind of irrelevant. Suddenly, we would be back, on a more cosmic scale, to those Europeans of 1500, who suddenly realized that there was a big unknown world out there for the taking. And we would be just as ignorant about it as those sixteenth-century Europeans were about America.

If you don't like antigravity, try matter teleportation. You stand in a box, and you are re-created (and simultaneously destroyed) someplace else, all at the speed of light, since the electronic system to do this would move at this speed. What kind of world would exist if we could teleport living things, along with freight, is too far out for our imaginations. But you could go anyplace (including all the planets, presumably) anytime you felt like it. Anyone for a quick weekend on Mars—and remember, with all those apes doing the work, the weekend will last five or six days.

Just to get back to more mundane things, we can look at some really practical problems which we need to solve. Since our freedom instruments need so much energy, and since hydrocarbon burning to get energy in usable form is so polluting, some new form of nonpolluting energy would be most welcome. It also would enable us to expand the use of freedom instruments to the whole world.

Really cheap food would be another major breakthrough, since we now spend a lot of energy in farming what we need to feed people. This one actually would be much more exciting for poor countries, where rapid population growth and low productivity makes this problem critical. We have already seen it happen, in the form of the green revolution, the development of hybrid varieties of wheat and rice, which have increased yields per acre threefold or more since 1968 in many foreign countries. But how about nonfarming farming, where food is manufactured cheaply, in factories? Not only would we then free millions of acres of land for other purposes, but our food supply would become much more reliable as well. And once again, our options would expand.

You can have fun thinking up new possibilities. There is a whole academic field of futurology which tries to work out such developments. But what is most likely is something no one expects. Some new development totally unforeseen will occur, which will tend to make our options even more explosively varied than they now are. Such an occurrence may be totally new and unimagined, or it may stem from a development of something already happening, but as yet commercially undeveloped.

These technological developments are the exciting ones for most people, and they are the most fun to speculate about. Yet some of the more important developments in the future will deal with less glamorous problems. People tend to solve problems once they see the relevance and importance of them. Thus men and women now in their fifties can remember the Great Depression. In the 1930s, no one knew what to do about such catastrophes. But smart people went to work on the problem, and now know how to avoid depressions. Even a journeyman economist can give quite valid advice these days on how to avoid disaster. If this seems irrelevant, you ought to know that because we have not had a Great Depression in the past thirty years, your income, along with every man, woman, and child in these United States, is a thousand dollars higher than it would have been otherwise, and that kind of money can buy a lot of freedom instruments. In 2084, a young person will be very impatient with all those fifty-year-olds who keep mumbling about inflation, petty wars, big, uncontrollable organizations, and all the rest. Why, that's ancient history.

Finally, we should not overlook the tremendous progress being made in management. The things that do work well these days are private, profit-oriented companies. They know how to get things done, and the very existence of hundreds of millions of freedom instruments suggests one dimension of their success. More progress is to come, and more efficiencies will be made. Possibilities for management improvement outside the field of business, as in medical delivery-service systems, government agencies, and education, are enormous, and lots of brilliant people are working on improvements all the time. We now see near chaos in too many public and nonprofit organizations, because they cannot seem to get their managerial houses in order; by 2084 they will be very significantly improved. Such advances often seem trivial and mundane, unworthy of serious notice, but in the end, having some high-powered technology or science is useless unless the managers and administrators know how to use it wisely and well. And the possibilities for improvement along these lines are greater than those for science and technology.

One thing is sure—if new technological gadgets which yield more options and more freedom are made, they will sell, and people will begin using them very rapidly. Cost is a key problem—the real advantages of the existing freedom instruments stems largely from the fact that almost any modestly affluent family can afford them. If our next nifty antigravity gadget costs $42 million and is as big as a factory, it won't get bought much—but if it is car size and sells for $1,375, f.o.b. Cleveland, then brace yourself for some massive changes in a hurry.

What are the odds on any of this, plus lots of things already dreamed up, but as yet unrealized? Who knows? What were the odds on transistors, lasers, computers, or for that matter, telephones, X rays, or any other unexpected discovery? Things happen, often in ways we never really foresee. Every so often, some one comes up with something really new, often elegantly simple (like a transistor), and we can expect something more in the future. Maybe we won't live to see it—maybe the next generation will be the one to have the pleasure. Then again, maybe we will. But it's sort of fun to consider that all that has happened so far is just a prelude to the real freedom which is going to come and make every concept we have about the way the world works look just plain silly.

If this seems too far out, ponder sticking old Lem from 1884 into the world of 1973. Nothing in his philosophy or experience could have prepared him for what he would find, and that was only ninety-one years ago. When you're ninety-one, you may be seeing and experiencing things that we can't imagine either. Indeed, giving what has happened, along with the steadily accelerating pace of scientific advance, it will probably be an even stranger world.